BAZENTIN RIDGE

Battleground Europe

BAZENTIN RIDGE

EDWARD HANCOCK

Series editor
Nigel Cave

LEO COOPER

an imprint of
Pen & Sword Books Limited
47 Church Street, Barnsley, South Yorkshire S70 2AS

ISBN 0 85052 782 1

A CIP catalogue of this book is available
from the British Library

Printed by CPI UK

*For up-to-date information on other titles produced under the Leo Cooper imprint,
please telephone or write to:*
Pen & Sword Books Ltd, FREEPOST, 47 Church Street
Barnsley, South Yorkshire S70 2AS
Telephone 01226 734222

Rebuilding the village – Bazentin-le-Petit – circa 1923.

CONTENTS

Bazentin-le-Petit – Rue LaMarck – circa 1930.

To my father.

My father, Robert Hancock was born on 1st January 1880 in Worksop, Nottinghamshire. On leaving school at the age of twelve he entered farm service, receiving each Michaelmas day, the payment of a very small annual sum from which to buy his personal needs for the year. In addition, all his meals 'heaps of fresh vegetables', his working clothes, and a small attic room were provided. He always spoke very warmly about this period of his life and his experiences at Windmill Farm, but in 1898 circumstances decreed a change and he accepted an offer to join the building trade, and remained in the construction business for the rest of his working life.

On 5th September 1914, he volunteered for Kitchener's Army, and the following day reported to the Leicestershire Regiment Depot at Glen Parva Barracks, Leicester, and joined 'The Tigers.' On the 12th September the 9th Battalion was formed, into which my father was drafted, and on the 24th the battalion arrived in Aldershot, first for 'individual training, squad, and platoon drill' at Bourley Camp, and then for further 'company and battalion training' in Talavera Barracks. On the 23rd February a route march was started which took the battalion to Kent, where it stayed in the New Romney and Dymchurch area, for 'the least productive of periods due to the lack of equipment and suitable training ground'. The Battalion was inspected, at Maidstone, for the second time by Field-Marshal Lord Kitchener at whose imploring behest the majority had volunteered in the wave of patriotic fervour which had swept the country. Entraining for No 10 Camp, Perham Down, Tidworth, on 8th April 1915, the 9th Battalion joined there the 6th,7th, and 8th Battalions, to form the 110 (Leicestershire) Brigade and to complete training, ready to embark for France fully and fighting fit in July 1915.

Just prior to the departure, H.M. King George V inspected the Battalion. The next occasion on which my father would see the King would be at Buckingham Palace on 21st November 1917 when he received the Military Cross, an honour, which he maintained was deserved by 'all the poor buggers who were in the bloody place' and, of which he was rightly proud.

The literally bloody place was, of course, Bazentin le Petit, a place of which I have always seemed fully aware, but whose name was rarely uttered within earshot during my childhood. My father died in 1970 after enjoying a full and healthy life surrounded by a loving family, although the privations of the 30's, the stresses and restrictions of war in the 40's, and the rationing of the 50's, hardly allowed fulfilment of the promise of a world fit for heroes.

Much respected by those who knew him, I remember my father as a fair and strong-minded man, outspoken when the need arose, and a champion of the underdog's cause. Calm, unhurried and patient, he was nevertheless haunted throughout his life by spectres from Bazentin. Sometimes during troublesome dreams he would curse his demons and shout desperate orders out loudly. On

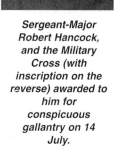

Sergeant-Major Robert Hancock, and the Military Cross (with inscription on the reverse) awarded to him for conspicuous gallantry on 14 July.

other occasions frantic nightmares invaded his sleep, disturbing my mother and, now and then, alarming visitors.

On the 14th July 1916, Company Sergeant Major Robert Hancock as senior remaining rank, collected together and assumed command of a group of men from various units scattered about the north of the clearing by Bazentin le Petit Wood, organised a defensive line and, at great personal risk, rallied the fight against a strong German counterattack attempting to break through from the north. He was wounded during this hectic action, but later, on the arrival of reinforcements, moved westwards to join an operation to clear the north west sector of the wood. A considerable number of his fellows and friends were maimed and killed around him during the mayhem of this, and the following two days. Much later in life, with great sorrow, he still clearly remembered them. A constant reminder struck on the 16th July when he was hit and wounded a second time, and consequently repatriated. Two separate pieces of shrapnel remained lodged in his left leg throughout his life.

After some days in the No. 3 Canadian War Hospital Boulogne, a period of convalescence followed at the War Hospital in Bagthorpe, Nottingham. Invited to a tea party for wounded soldiers, given at The Homestead, Bulwell, he there met an old friend from his schooldays, and some months later married her youngest sister, Gladys Reeves Stenton, then aged nineteen.

When father was posted to Northern Command Depot, Ripon, in January 1917, on attachment to the Durham Light Infantry, they rented a cottage in the grounds of Fountains Abbey where they stayed until his discharge from the Army in May 1919.

Born the last of eight children when my father was fifty-six years old, opportunities to satisfy my curiosity as a child about his heroism, and my later growing interest in the details surrounding his decoration, I regret, I did not pursue with sufficient zeal. Amongst the time consuming developments of my own life, and, I tell myself, out of respect for my father's reticence to talk about the subject, details as to what happened on that fateful day in that bloody battle were not related, occasions for discourse were allowed to pass, lost

opportunities which I now rue, and which, I am quite sure, would he.

From a specific interest in my father's involvement in the action at Bazentin, my passion grew to encompass the whole puzzle of those enthusiastic volunteers for war who fought with such zest for self sacrifice from the trenches, the patriotic duty displayed by practically the whole of the population through-out the period of the Great War, and the far reaching changes which followed.

A three-year period starting in the spring of 1995, living in northern France with my wife and baby daughter, allowed me time to investigate on the spot answers to many of the questions I had posed over the years. The collection of notes from that time expanded into this volume after a meeting with Nigel Cave, whose encouragement and assistance has proved invaluable.

This book is written in tribute to my father and all who similarly served; with a profound sadness at the inevitability of the awful human suffering in the clashes of war; with wonder at the incredible bravery and heroics of the combatants; and with humility remembering the blind, crippled, and shell-shocked men of my father's generation, who were still suffering terrible consequences many years after the conflict.

EDWARD DAVID HANCOCK. LOUGHBOROUGH, LEICESTERSHIRE. JULY 2000.

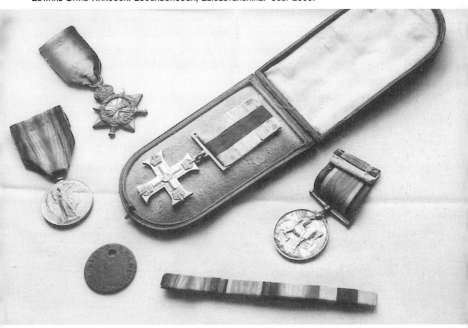

Introduction by Series Editor

When I started the *Battleground Europe* series several years ago, one of the battlefields that I was most keen to cover was Bazentin le Petit. I had a very personal interest, as it was here that my grandfather, serving with 7/Leicesters, part of 110 Brigade, participated in his first major battle. His brigade had been in France for almost exactly a year, but most of that time was spent in the tedium – but danger – of holding the line around Berles and Bienvilliers, just to the north of what was to become the battlefield of the Somme, 1916.

My grandfather died in 1961 when I was seven years old. I have very clear and very fond memories of him, but obviously never spoke to him of his battle experiences. He remained in the army after the war – and, indeed, through the Second. He had joined up in 1914 from a textile factory where he was a clerk. He had been pondering the possibility of emigrating to Argentina and had set about learning Spanish – but instead he joined the flood of young men rushing to join the Colours. His administrative skills served him in good stead and he rose rapidly through the ranks, ending up as the youngest RQMS up to that time in the history of the British army.

One important legacy from his time in the army was a short diary, which he wrote up in the post-war years whilst serving with the Leicesters in India. It was that diary, along with the bound volumes of the War Illustrated and Bruce Bairnsfather's cartoons, which his father had collected for him, that led to my deep interest in the Great War,

An opportunity came to visit the old front line when my parents were posted to Germany; it was a long weekend tour that encompassed Waterloo, Ypres and the Somme. This was my father's first return since he was taken by his father on a battlefield tour shortly before the Second World War, at a time when he was my age. Sharing this great interest has been a great pleasure, and we have made regular annual

Wrecked howitzer – Bazentin-le-Petit Wood.

pilgrimages to the battlefields ever since I got a car. One memorable year we followed my grandfather through his diary and were amazed to find relics mentioned in his journal. At Berles there still remained a small well in a field *(well water handy)*; whilst down at Chateau Marzilly, near Rheims, there was writing on the wall dating from the brigade's time there in 1918: *these stoves are ready to use* – just the sort of thing an RQMS would have had done.

Fortune brought me in touch with Edward Hancock, and who could have been a more suitable choice to write this book if I could not? The writing on Bazentin has always been thin on the ground, overshadowed to a large extent by the prolonged struggle for the nearby High Wood. This very comprehensive account should serve to put that right and help to ensure that the Leicestershire men of Kitchener's army – such as the CSM (Perkins) mentioned in a diary extract below – are not forgotten and that the memory, like old soldiers, does not simply 'fade away'.

July 14th

Brigade attacked this morning at 3.25 a.m. and took Bazentin Wood, Bazentin le Petit, and Bazentin le Grand. 146 men of my company killed or missing. CSM of my company had his leg shot off, displayed great courage in rallying the men. He died later in hospital. I lost most of my friends this day. Went up to the front with rations, and the most ghastly sights met our eyes. Dead men every few yards and the place smells stale with the slaughter which has been going on for the past fourteen days. The place is a very hell, with the whistling and crashing of shells, bursting shrapnel, and the rattle of machine guns. The woods we had taken had not yet been cleared, and there were pockets of Germans with machine guns still holding out and doing some damage. A sergeant sinks to the ground beside me with a bullet hole in his shoulder. Lucky man. It is not likely to prove fatal. It is too clean and it means a few months in Blighty for him.

July 15th

The Germans counter attack but were repulsed.

July 16th

Battalion came out of the line, and bivouaced at Mametz. I had to call the roll of the company, and this was a heart-breaking business. The answer to most of the names was "killed". All men who were not definitely known to have been killed were posted as missing. For this we had to rely on the knowledge of the few survivors of course.

Arthur Charles Cave
RQMS 7 Leicesters. July 1916.

Author's Introduction

The writing of this book to me will never be complete. Each day something arises which may, or may not, increase the content and contribute to the closer understanding of the steps taken by those fighting and how they fought across the ground in 1916, but for the book to be published deadlines must be met or, with apologies to the publishers just missed, and the question becomes not what is to be added but what must be cut.

My first visit to the Somme battlefield was in 1965, a detour during a business trip from Paris to Belgium. Although the weather was wet and misty I remember being deeply impressed by the feeling of familiarity and ease and, during many visits since, my appreciation and accord with the French countryside in this area has continued to increase. Many friends and associates have felt the same way and repeatedly visit the area. The pleasant and rolling countryside with well defined woods and copses, has recovered over the years almost exactly to its pre 1916 configuration and it is difficult to imagine now the utter devastation which rolled inexorably across the land, spewing thousands of tons of explosives and scrap metal and leaving thousands dead.

The part of the conflict covered in this book is a continuation of the great Somme Battle which began on 1st July 1916. The south of the attack front pushed the opposing German line back far enough to secure Montauban and Mametz, and two days later Fricourt was occupied. A bloody and slogging engagement then pushed the Germans back further gaining Mametz Wood and Contalmaison, and setting up circumstances favourable to pressing on with the planned attack against Bazentin Ridge. The divisions involved had been fighting since the first day, alternating between attack and recuperation, but this would be the first time the New Army Battalions had undertaken a full scale night attack. The German front line here was their second line prior to the British success of the 1st July, and the Switchline was being quickly developed and fortified as the second line of defence.

The Battlefield Europe Books covering the surrounding areas each written, as is this, with a passionate interest in the subject, will increase appreciation and understanding of the struggles. The cemeteries of the area, beautifully maintained by the Commonwealth War Graves Commission, each have their own character and atmosphere, occasionally brooding and dark, but mostly light and airy, places for quiet contemplation in peace and tranquillity. The names of the small villages in the region have been repeated many times on memorials and commemorations to individuals and are known throughout the Commonwealth.

Maps reproduced in this book annotated with troop positions and routes, are 1:10000 scale trench maps courtesy of the Imperial War Museum. The Western Front was gridded into large squares or rectangles named and identified by letters (in this book Longueval 57C SW3 – S). Each grid was subdivided into 1000 yard squares identified by number, then into four sub squares, the top two numbered a and b, the bottom two, c and d, which in turn were subdivided into 50 yard squares read from the bottom left corner, horizontal first and then vertical. ie. map reference S.7.d.3.4. is square 7, right hand corner sub-square d, 3 x 50 yards horizontal (east), 4 x 50 yards vertical (north). By subdividing into half squares positions could be very precisely denoted.

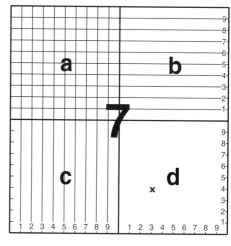

The basic organisation of the British Army was that each division consisted of three infantry brigades, plus two field artillery brigades, a howitzer brigade, a heavy artillery brigade and a pioneer brigade, with two field engineer companies, a signal company and a field ambulance company. Each infantry brigade consisted of four battalions, plus brigade HQ. Each battalion consisted of four companies plus HQ, 240 men in each company when at full strength, plus machine gun section, and support troops (stretcher-bearers, signals etc.). Each company consisted of four platoons split into four sections.

The German organisation was similar. Each division consisting of two infantry brigades and one artillery brigade, plus cavalry, pioneers, and medical corps. Each brigade consisted of two regiments split into three battalions each of four companies plus a machine gun company.

The variety of arms used by the clashing armies is too extensive to describe here, but many books specialising in weapons, dress, transport, in fact in all technical aspects of the conflict are available for the serious student and for reference.

Acknowledgements

A considerable number of sources have been used in the compilation of this book. My first acknowledgement is to those who chronicled the information in the first place, the writers of the battalion diaries, army records, and personal diaries of the time, and individual accounts related since.

I would like to thank; all in Museums and Records offices who have contributed their knowledge and have helped with so much patience and enthusiasm; members of the Western Front Association who have wittingly or unwittingly assisted; walking chums of the Somme, especially George Taylor and Leslie McHugh; Matthew Richardson author of *The Tigers*, and all friends and acquaintances who have contributed snippets of information and assistance; and especially to my wife for her forbearance and sympathetic listening over the years of gestation.

In particular I thank the staffs of the Imperial War Museum, the Commonwealth War Graves Commission, and the Public Records Office. Also Taylor Picture Library. DD Gibson for the successful searches, Mme Dolivet, Mme Huguette Dupire and the Maire of Bazentin for local information and assistance, Squire de Lisle of Quenby Hall for his generosity in allowing me access to private family archives, and the Read family for allowing reproduction of passages from *Of Those We Loved,* and to Chester Read for the additional help and information.

Thanks to Faber and Faber Ltd., for permission to quote from *Siegfried Sassoon's Memoirs of an Infantry Officer*, and to Penguin Books Ltd., for permission to quote from *The Somme* by Lyn Macdonald.

Errors or omissions are entirely mine for which I apologise.

I must finally and especially record my greatest thanks to Nigel Cave, the editor of the series, whose close co-operation in the writing of this book has ensured a successful conclusion, and whose editorial expertise and guidance proved invaluable.

Advice to Tourers

The approaches to this part of the Somme battlefield are given at the beginning of the tours section. The Bazentins are small villages – Bazentin le Grand is, in effect, only a large farm. Facilities such as somewhere to eat may be found in the nearby village of Longueval and at the South African Memorial on the east end of it.

For touring purposes the maps in the book should be sufficient; but the 1:25000 Blue Series 2408 E (Bray sur Somme) covers the immediate area; also useful for this book would be 2407 E (Bapaume). For more general navigation uses I would strongly recommend number 4 in the Green Series (1:100000), Laon Arras.

This is a fascinating part of the Somme battlefield and one which is still relatively quiet. Most tour buses head for the South African Memorial and then continue on elsewhere to the major Somme sites. There are other books in this series which should be of immediate relevance, notably Mike Stedman's Fricourt-Mametz and Michael Renshaw's Mametz Wood. There have been two excellent books on the fighting in Mametz Wood (Mametz, by Colin Hughes) and High Wood (The Hell They Called High Wood, by Terry Norman).

Although it is in a different season to the fighting on 14th July, I have found the early months of the year an excellent time to come and get good views of the fighting area here: the trees are bare, the fields are fallow or the crops are in their early stages; and the weather can be excellent. This is a battle which took place in the open, in considerable woods and in buildings – a very complex fighting environment.

Some advice on what to take with you is in the touring section; but always have a small rucksack, water, camera and spare films and batteries, a notebook and pencils, waterproof and reasonably stout shoes. Please respect the livelihood of the people who live here – do not block tracks, do not trespass into woods and leave all munitions well alone. The accompanying photograph, taken in October 2000 at Martinpuich, illustrates how much in the way of munitions still surface

here.

There is a very useful and extensive bookshop within the refreshment area at the South African Memorial with a whole range of useful publications. Note that it is closed on Mondays and public holidays and from the end of November to the early days of February. For those who are seeking information about relatives, the Commonwealth War Graves Commission at Maidenhead (O1628 634221) can help with details of those killed in the war – or go straight to their website.

Ensure that you have insured both yourself and the car; and that your tetanus booster is up to date. Theft from cars is not unusual (especially at the bigger sites), so please take the usual standard precautions. There is a large range of accommodation now on the Somme, and finding somewhere should not be too difficult, so long as the period around 1st July is avoided. There is a helpful tourist information office in the Basilica Square in Albert. B and B accommodation in the area includes:

Martinpuich; Colin and Lisa Gillard, 54 Grand Rue
Tel: 321 50 18 87.
Grandcourt: Mme Bellengez, 9 Rue de Beaucourt
Tel: 322 74 81 58.
Auchonvillers/ Beaumont Hamel: Mike and Julie Renshaw, Les Galets, Route de Beaumont, Auchonvillers
Tel: 322 76 28 79
Auchonvillers: Avril Williams, 10 Rue Delattre,
Tel: 322 76 23 66.
Courcelette: Paul Reed, 39 Grand Rue
Tel: 322 74 01 35.

Hotels convenient for the area include:
The Royal Picardie, Route d'Amiens 80300 Albert
Tel 322 75 37 00.
Hotel de la Basilique, 3 Rue Gambetta, 80300 Albert
Tel 322 75 04 71.
Le Relais Fleuri, 56 Ave Faidherbe, 80300 Albert
Tel 32 75 08 11
Grande Hotel de la Paix, 43 Rue Victor Hugo, Albert
Tel 322 75 01 64
Within a reasonable driving distance both Arras and Amiens have a number of larger modern hotels.

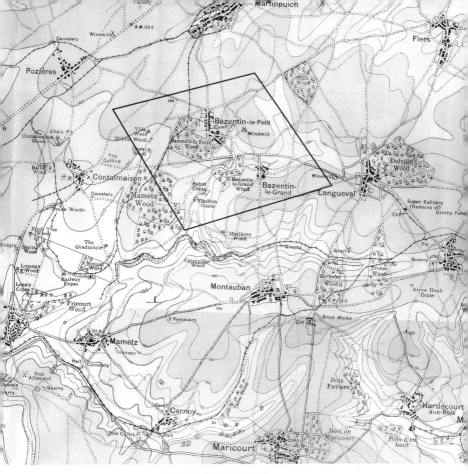

LIST OF MAPS

INTRODUCTION

At 03.20 hours, in the indistinct light of the mist-clouded early dawn on the morning of Friday 14 July 1916, the bombardment on the German second line defences, increased to an unprecedented intensity along the 6000 yard front from west of Bazentin le Petit Wood to Longueval and continued for five searing minutes. This heralded the start of what is officially known as The Battle of Bazentin Ridge.

Although this ferocious battle, short in duration, started with a surprise attack, it was not totally unexpected by the German command. In fact, German war records of the time detail the plans which were being effected to strengthen the defence resources on this front following the advances by the allies in this sector since the start of the Somme battle on the 1st July 1916 and the recent bloody capture of much of Mametz Wood.

The battle plan of XV Corps, devised by Fourth Army commander, General Rawlinson, with the agreement of his field infantry commanders, was that, in secrecy and silence, and under the cover of darkness, four divisions of British infantry (9th, 3rd, 7th and 21st) with support troops, were to be in position ready to storm the German second line positions immediately on cessation of the short, intensive artillery barrage. This was received with some reservation by the Commander in Chief and his staff, and scoffed at by General Foch, the commander of the French forces immediately south of the British Fourth Army.

Fourth Army commander, General Rawlinson.

The innovative short barrage (suggested by the artillery commanders of the 3rd and 9th Divisions) carried out by all massed available guns of XIII and XV Corps, was followed by an equally innovative creeping barrage using HE shell only (18-pdr, 4.5-inch and medium howitzers), which proved entirely satisfactory and relatively easy for the infantry to follow.

The first objectives were the capture of the German front and support trenches, from Delville Wood through Longueval, to the south of Bazentin le Grand village and wood and across the south of Bazentin le Petit Wood, to link with III Corps (1st Division), whose

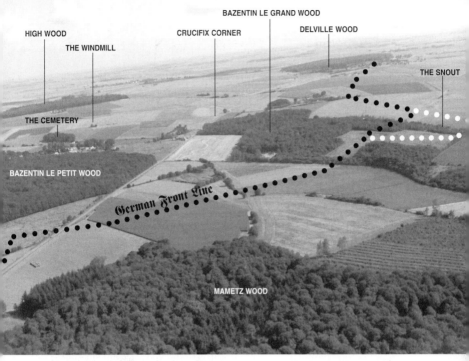

An aerial view of the battlefields from above Mametz Wood with the line of the German front line trench indicated.

objective was to capture Contalmaison Villa, thereby securing the left flank. The second objectives immediately following were to secure Delville Wood, the remainder of Longueval village, and the two Bazentin woods and villages.

This operation would enable an immediate assault on High Wood, and the capture of this strategic strong point that lies on the crest of the ridge north west of Longueval. Just how close this operation came to complete success will be evident as the account of the action unfolds. This book covers the action undertaken by the 7th and 21st Divisions, and the adjoining 9 Brigade, and their assaults on the Bazentin woods and villages, the action of the 3rd and 9th Divisions east of the Bazentins to Delville Wood will be, or have been, covered in other books in the series.

Chapter One

A DARING SCHEME: PLANNING AND PREPARATIONS

The plan devised by General Rawlinson, commanding the British Fourth Army, and his corps commanders for the assault on the second German line of defences: using surprise tactics; using four battalions to attack a 6,000 yard front before dawn, having assumed their forward positions silently, and in secrecy, and in full battle order during the preceding night; and ready to assault the opposing trenches after a short artillery barrage, was not initially accepted by his Commander in Chief, General Sir Douglas Haig.

The British 'new army' battalions assigned to this attack, in the opinion of the Commander-in-Chief, were not sufficiently experienced to undertake such a complicated night operation as that proposed. The counterproposal from GHQ was that the Bazentin part of the front (where the distance between the British positions and the German second line defences was shortest) be attacked by the 7th and 21st Divisions some two hours before sunset and, after the successful achievement of objectives, the remainder of the front be then attacked in flank eastwards from the Bazentins, whilst the 3rd and 9th Divisions moved northwards in daylight the following morning.

On 8 July 1916 General Rawlinson issued the preparatory order to attack the German second line, albeit certain key points – Contalmaison, Mametz Wood, and Trones Wood – necessary to facilitate the planned attack, were not yet secured.

As result of the freedom in the air which the Royal Flying Corps

Big guns moving up to the front.

were enjoying at this time, the German second and third line positions were photographed carefully, and the ground objectives reconnoitred.

On 11 July a bombardment by the artillery of XIII, XV and III Corps on the German positions began, concentrating particularly on the lines of approach and key reserve points, effectively hindering the forward movements of vital replenishments and troops to the German front line. The progress of ammunition limbers to the British front positions was not particularly affected by German artillery action, (aerial observation being denied by the supremacy of the Royal Flying Corps), but the poor state of the ground between the forward dumps and the guns resulted in each round trip taking up to six hours. In addition there was a general shortfall in the quantity of ammunition available. The consequent restrictions limited the number of rounds allocated per day for the scheduled two day bombardment to: 25 per 15 inch; 50 per 9.2 inch; 110 per 8 inch; and 250 per 6 inch.

When the start of the operation was postponed the total quantity of ammunition allocated was increased to cover the additional day's requirements. As well as ammunition, all manner of battle materials were brought up by night and stored in the area of Caterpillar Valley; the dumps, in the open, remained undetected and, largely undamaged.

In spite of GHQ doubts about the Corps plan, in the absence of contrary direction, the Divisional Commanders of the 3rd, 7th , 9th and 21st Divisions continued with preparations for a night attack in accordance with their agreed strategy, hoping that their plan would be finally agreed by GHQ.

General Rawlinson accepted and approved the arrangements for the night attack by the 9th Division (Major-General WT Furse) and the 3rd Division (Major General JAL Haldane) and wrote privately to Sir Douglas Haig urging acceptance of the plan. He stated that the alternative plan proposed would greatly reduce the width of the attack front and therefore allow the concentration of German artillery fire,

that the element of surprise would be greatly reduced, and that to change the direction of attack and to have two directions of assault would pose very difficult manoeuvres under battle conditions.

This letter, which was received by General Haig early on the morning of 12 July, was augmented at 8 am by a final telephoned appeal from Major General AA Montgomery (Chief of Staff to General Rawlinson) to General Kiggell, the Chief of the General Staff. As a result of these last minute pleas, and encouraged by a report from his Artillery Adviser (Major-General JFN Birch) advising that the artillery was successfully meeting objectives and that a pre-dawn attack would leave the light of a full day to exploit the success, the Commander-in-Chief replied to General Rawlinson that he was now prepared to agree to the Fourth Army plan, and was sending General Kiggell personally to convey his decision agreeing to the plan for night assembly and dawn assault by XIII and XV Corps as proposed, on condition that the flanks were first secured by the capture of Trones and Mametz woods.

On the 12 and 13 July the British Fourth Army Headquarters received repeated telephone calls from the French Sixth Army Headquarters requesting, with increasing insistence, that the planned attack, regarded by the French Command as being foolhardy and doomed to failure, be cancelled.

On the evening of the 13th, General Balfourier, Commander of the French XX Corps,

> a much beloved old gentleman, who still wore the French
> uniform of the Second Empire, complete with wide red trousers,

sent over the British liaison officer, Captain EL Spears, with a final message, pointing out that success was impossible using the inexperienced troops available for the planned night attack. Major-General Montgomery retorted,

> Tell General Balfourier, with my compliments, that if we are not
> on Longueval Ridge at eight tomorrow morning I will eat my hat.

Little did Montgomery know that his remark would be repeated verbatim to the General.

Although some details, and certainly the date, were amended, XV Corps Operation Order No.17 dated 11 July states that the attack by the 7th and 21st Divisions would start at 3.25 am on 14 July 1916 (was originally planned for the 13th), that the attack would be made in conjunction with a French attack to the immediate south of the British positions (although in fact this did not happen) and that III Corps would establish a strong defensive flank from the south west corner of Bazentin le Petit wood. An addendum added that Contalmaison Villa

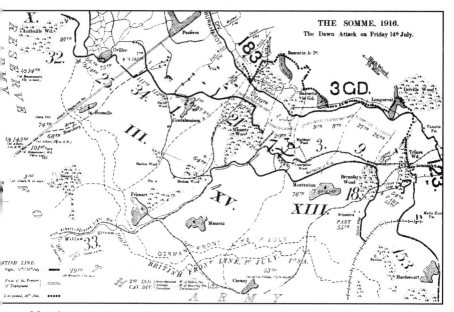

Map 1.

was to be secured by III Corps at the earliest possible moment, and that the attack was bound to that of XIII Corps (3rd and 9th Divisions) on the right flank.

An intense barrage on the German front line trench system of the usual thirty minutes duration was planned but, at the behest of the artillery commanders of the 3rd Division (Brigadier-General EWM Powell) and the 9th Division (Brigadier-General HH Tudor) was amended to be of five minutes only, but of an unprecedented intensity. The standard thirty minute procedure, they insisted, would not only

Map 2: German account of the battle of 14 July 1916.

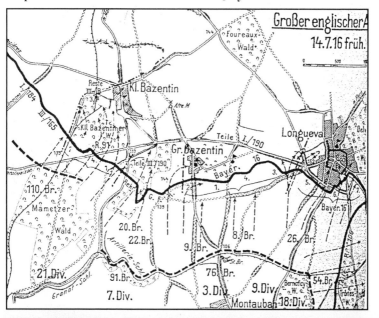

serve as warning to the enemy of the impending attack but would encourage retaliatory fire. The opening barrage was furthermore to be followed by an innovative creeping barrage very closely co-ordinated with the infantry advance.

The dividing line between the 3rd and 21st Divisions would be the road running between the north east corner of Mametz Wood and the south east corner of Bazentin le Petit Wood and thence along the eastern edge of Bazentin le Petit Wood, and along the Bazentin le Petit – Martinpuich road running through the village. The 7th Division attack would link from the 3rd Division boundary along the western edge of Bazentin le Grand Wood and extend west to include the village of Bazentin le Grand.

Objectives of the divisions as stated in the XV Corps Operation Order No 17 were as follows:

21st Division. – 110 Brigade.
First objective: *To capture enemy defences (front and support trenches) between the line of the road running from the east corner of Mametz Wood to Bazentin Le Petit (road inclusive) and the west edge of Bazentin le Petit Wood.*

Second objective :
(a) *To capture the portion of BAZENTIN LE PETIT VILLAGE West of the BAZENTIN LE PETIT – MARTINPUICH road (exclusive), and to capture BAZENTIN LE PETIT WOOD.*

(b) *To establish themselves on the line of the northern edge of the VILLAGE (joining up there with the 7th Division) - the road thence to CONTALMAISON VILLA - along the Northern edge of BAZENTIN LE PETIT WOOD - Western edge of WOOD to the South West corner of the WOOD.* [The road to which this paragraph in the order refers was a continuation of the track which starts at the crossroads at the north of Bazentin le Petit village on the left of the Royal Engineers memorial, and which now bears left down the west side of the wood. In 1916 this road continued straight linking with the road from Contalmaison to Farm de la Trouee at the site of what was Contalmaison Villa.]

(c) *To establish connection with III Corps (1st Division) at S7 D 31. (South west corner of Bazentin le Petit Wood).*

7th Division – 20 & 22 Brigades.
First objective: *To capture enemy defences (front and support trenches) between a line joining S 15 a 1½ 4 to first E of BAZENTIN LE GRAND WOOD and the line of the road running from the East corner of MAMETZ WOOD to BAZENTIN LE PETIT (road inclusive).* [On the right of the 21st Division and to a line from east of Bazentin le Grand Wood to Marlborough Wood adjoining the 3rd Division troops.]

Second objective:
(a) *To capture BAZENTIN LE GRAND WOOD– the portion of BAZENTIN LE PETIT VILLAGE East of the BAZENTIN LE PETIT – MARTINPUICH road and CEMETERY.*

(b) *To establish the line – North East corner of BAZENTIN LE GRAND WOOD –*

MAMETZ WOOD   MARLBOROUGH WOOD   BAZENTIN LE PETIT WOOD   BAZENTIN LE GRAND WOOD   BAZENTIN LE GR[A]ND VILLAGE

CEMETERY (inclusive) Northern edge of
BAZENTIN LE PETIT VILLAGE as far as the BAZENTIN LE PETIT –
MARTINPUICH Road (inclusive) and to join up with the 21st Division.

(c) To establish connection with XIII Corps (3rd Division troops) at
S15 a 2 9½. [North east of Bazentin le Grand Wood.]

The objectives of the 3rd Division of XIII Corps adjoining XV Corps front were:

9 Brigade:

First Objective: *To capture and consolidate the enemy's support line from S.15.b.5.1 to about S.15.a.3.1 in touch with 7th Division.*

Second Objective: *To capture and fortify the village of BAZENTIN LE GRAND.*

Third Objective: *To establish a defensive line from Road Junction at N.E. Corner of BAZENTIN LE GRAND WOOD along track or ditch to S.15.a.9.9 and thence along road to S.9.d.5.0.*

Fourth Objective: *To keep in touch with and assist the attack of 7th Division on BAZENTIN LE GRAND WOOD and, if necessary, to establish a defensive flank from elbow of trench at S.15.1Ω.4 to point where MARLBORO TRENCH crosses track about S.20.b.4.9 and thence South along MARLBORO TRENCH.*

8 Brigade was to attack the German's support trenches from S.15.b.5.1 westwards to S 16.b.6.5 and then to advance forwards to establish a defensive line from S.9.d.5.0 adjoining 9 Brigade then west to link with the 9th Division at S.16.b.6.5.

So the plan for The Battle of the Bazentin Ridge was set, or at least the part with which this book is concerned. Considering that the whole battle involved a logistical and military organisation almost as complicated as that for the action of 1st July, a number of other instructions advised in XV Corps Order, and action in other parts of the battleground, are relevant.

110 Brigade had been transferred from the 37th Division to the 21st Division the result of the request to Fourth Army HQ for fresh troops as urgent replacements for battalions depleted during the constant action on and since 1 July. It had been in reserve to supplement the 46th Division, but due to the stalemate at Gommecourt had been unused. In readiness for the attack, during the night of 10/11 July, the 21st Division (110 Brigade) relieved the 17th Division in the area of Quadrangle Support Trench between Contalmaison and Mametz Wood – the 17th Division had fought fiercely and with heavy losses to secure the ground, and were withdrawn to reserve.

Having withdrawn from its reserve position just north of Gommecourt, the 110 Leicestershire Brigade moved south to join the

The attack front of 14 July – Battle of Bazentin Ridge viewed from the south.

| HIGH WOOD | CATERPILLAR VALLEY CEMETERY | DELVILLE WOOD LONGUEVAL |

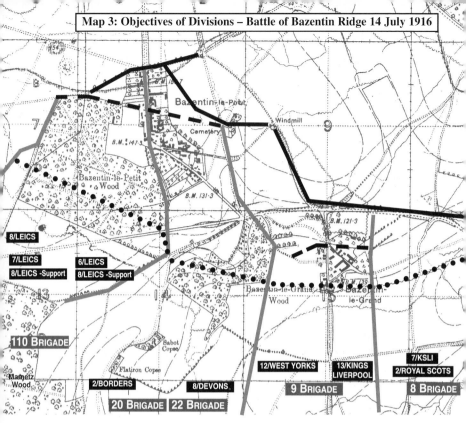

On the map:

8/LEICS

7/LEICS
8/LEICS -Support

6/LEICS
8/LEICS -Support

110 BRIGADE

Mametz Wood

Flatiron Copse

Sabot Copse

2/BORDERS

8/DEVONS

20 BRIGADE   22 BRIGADE

12/WEST YORKS

13/KINGS LIVERPOOL

9 BRIGADE

7/KSLI
2/ROYAL SCOTS

8 BRIGADE

Bazentin-le-Petit Wood

Bazentin-le-Grand Wood

Bazentin le-Grand

Bazentin-le-Petit

Windmill

Cemetery

21st Division. Dick Read expresses very delicately a brief insight into the thoughts of a private soldier who would shortly be thrown into the carnage of battle. He enlisted in the 8/Leicesters in 1914, and in 1917 was to be commissioned into the Royal Sussex Regiment. His book, *Of Those We Loved*, is a moving recollection of his service through the Great War, and a testament to all those who served. He reflected about the march and the move south:

> *Although we were not in a condition to properly appreciate it at the time, we could not help noticing that the countryside hereabouts was extremely interesting in character, contrasting sharply with the rolling expanses we had lately traversed. Hangest-sur-Somme appeared to me to be a charming old-world town, sleeping in the July sun, on a river among surroundings having real scenic quality. I could not help thinking – although lying wearily on the roadside verge, propped up by my heavy pack – that here was a peep at the real France that I had read about in books.*

> *Beyond Hangest we made slow progress. Our colonel and other mounted officers now shepherded us continually, each riding with several slung rifles. Even though carrying several*

rifles, Colonel Mignon made a fine figure of a soldier, sitting his horse as though part of it, his iron-grey military moustache upturned at the ends almost Kaiser-fashion.

We would have dropped in our tracks that day rather than have straggled. It would have been letting him down. Such an attitude may seem naïve and outdated to the youth of fifty years after. We knew in those moments that in Colonel Mignon and his officers we had real leaders. We all helped one another to get along, so that at length we hobbled into the village of Soues, where we found clean, sweet-smelling straw in a lovely old barn. We washed, ate...and then slept. [7]

Having spent three refreshing and happy days in Soues the battalion assembled on the morning of 11 July to be addressed and inspected by Colonel Mignon and the Adjutant, Captain Popham, prior to entraining for the front that evening.

Speaking slowly and deliberately, he told us that the 110th Leicestershire Brigade was about to take part in the great offensive on the Somme, and we should uphold the honour of our regiment and of our country. He asked us to remember that we were fighting as Englishmen, for all that Englishmen held dear. Finally he told us that the Leicestershire Regiment did not know the meaning of the word 'retreat', and as this would be the last opportunity he would have of addressing us for some time, he wished us good luck, and Godspeed.

During the night 11 /12 July the badly mauled 38th (Welsh) Division in the area extending from Mametz Wood and east to Marlborough Wood was relieved by the 7th Division, which itself had snatched barely five days respite from action, having had little time effectively to absorb 1400 officers and men from various regiments drafted in to replace earlier casualties.

Three cavalry divisions were ordered to readiness as from 4 am on 14 July, the 2nd Indian Cavalry Division being placed under orders of the G.O.C XIII Corps, with the capture of High Wood as their objective.

The IV Royal Flying Corps Brigade under Brigadier General ('Splash') Ashmore was responsible for the air operations of Fourth Army Corps. With headquarters located in the chateau at Bertangles, both the 3rd Corps Wing covering reconnaissance and artillery observation, and the 14th Fighter Wing operated out of Bertangles aerodrome. The number of British aeroplanes operating at the beginning of the Somme battle totalled, including reserves, 637, a substantial increase from the 270 at the end of March 1916. The foresight of planning this expansion enabled the RFC to establish the air superiority which proved vital in the Battle for Bazentin Ridge, flying low level contact patrols, liasing with and between infantry and artillery, directing artillery fire, removing enemy observation balloons, and in strafing and reconnaissance missions.

As a result of the fighting since 1 July, and subsequent accurate British artillery fire directed from the air by Royal Flying Corps observers, considerable losses and absence of accurate communications resulted in planned German counter-attacks on the Bazentin – Poziéres sector during the period from 7 to 13 July being at first postponed, then cancelled. At the same time the opposing German forces were undergoing considerable reorganisation.

A German Operation Order issued by 28th Reserve Division, dated 4 July 1916, referring to the improvement of positions, called for an immediate establishment of a second trench in the defence line (albeit at the time of issue relevant to the line through Contalmaison and Mametz Wood, and on to The Snout) and that the many undamaged

The FE2B, fullfilled a variety of roles, mainly long range reconnaissance, and as a general escort aircraft. Note the camera on the side of the aircraft.

RFC Officer relays target information to a RA Officer who orders guns to 'open fire', in front of Montauban July 1916

dug-outs be used not only for quartering troops, but be developed as strong points to ensure that enemy shellfire damage would not render the line indefensible. The flank fire from the strong points so established should prevent any breakthrough. The order further states:

> *Of particular importance for the defence is the quick building in of machine-guns behind the front defence line, which command the ground behind and which, with flank fire, can support each other, so that enemy forces which may at any point have temporarily broken through, may be held up by machine-gun fire from further advance.*

> *Furthermore, behind the front line the conversion of villages into strong points is of the greatest importance. Such villages are: Pozieres, Contalmaison, Bazentin le Petit, Bazentin le Grand, and Longueval.*

A German Regimental Order dated 9 July, taken from a prisoner of the 5th Company 122/Reserve Infantry Regiment, advises of the intention to restore battalions to full strength, and thanks officers in the line for their splendid reporting, which had, 'so far spared all surprises'. The order continues:

> *Also I must thank the men for their exemplary conduct during the strenuous days we have of late passed through. Nothing has affected that, not even the regrettable way in which the 2nd Battalion has been imperilled by the fire of our own artillery. This incident has been made by me the subject of rigorous and strict inquiry, especially the resulting loss of the lives of faithful comrades.*

> *God grant that the offensive power of our greatest enemies in this war may also in the future be stayed by our resistance.*

The German Army Command found the supply of replacement troops and equipment to the front was difficult under the incessant and accurate British artillery barrage and, on 13 July, in anticipation of a further British attack, command of the front between the River Ancre and

Longueval was allotted to *Group Armin* – the 183rd Division defending the Bazentins and the 3rd Guards Division defending east to Longueval.

General Sixt von Armin, who officially assumed command of the front at 9 am on 14 July, was faced with a critical situation. An official report states, 'there were no rear positions, no switches, no communication trenches, and that artillery had suffered severely'. All units were ordered to hold their positions at all costs pending reorganisation of the defences.

At the moment of the British attack, the German 7th Division was arriving to relieve the 183rd Division in the Bazentin le Petit Wood - Poziéres section. A further three regiments, the 26th, 27th, and 165th were ordered up to reinforce the whole Bazentin Ridge front including Longueval, and to occupy a second line in the rear, and additional units of the 185th, 17th Reserve, 26th Reserve, and 3rd Guards Divisions and some companies of the 55th Landwehr Regiment, which were resting in reserve positions, were ordered forward as further reinforcements, along with an additional 65 heavy guns and howitzers. Although this equivalent of fourteen battalions reinforced the fighting front, the formations were very mixed in composition, there having been no opportunity to properly reorganise replacements for the very heavy losses sustained in the recent defensive actions.

It is significant that the German offensive at Verdun ceased on 11 July by order of Falkenhayn, overall commander of the German armies, thereby fulfilling a prime reason for the Allied Somme offensive; but it also released resources to be deployed elsewhere, many to the Somme front.

Germans moving up to the front line in anticipation of the British attack.

Chapter Two

THE FORCES GATHER AND THE FINAL PREPARATIONS

The assault on the German support positions (now the front line positions) were to be lead by the 3rd and 9th Divisions of XIII Corps against the front between Delville Wood and Longueval and thence westwards to Bazentin le Grand, and by the 7th and 21st Divisions of XV Corps against Bazentin le Grand Wood and Bazentin le Petit Wood, village, and cemetery.

On the extreme right of the front, the 18th Division would link up with the 9th Division to form a defensive flank along the eastern edge of Trones Wood and with the French XX Corps near Maltz Horn Farm. On the extreme left of the front the 1st Division (III Corps) would form a defensive flank by seizing Contalmaison Villa in addition to securing the communication trench known as Pearl Alley, and would link up with the 21st Division at the south west corner of Bazentin le Petit Wood.

The great problem was whether the assaulting brigades, over 22,000 men, of the divisions detailed for the dawn attack, with their supporting troops, could be assembled in the darkness and formed up within 500 yards of the enemy not only without confusion but without the alarm being raised [the moon was full and set at 1.28 am- Summer Time - on the 14th]. *There were anxious moments at GHQ and at Fourth Army headquarters, until successive reports brought news of the undisturbed assembly of the various divisions; but this anxiety bore no comparison with the mental strain imposed on the brigade staffs,*

A substantial and well prepared German trench – before bombardment.

few of which boasted one trained staff officer, and on the engineer officers who arranged the details of the deployment.

Every possible precaution had been taken to ensure secrecy; it was known that the enemy possessed means of overhearing telephone conversations, and there was danger that he might have received some hint. On the morning of the thirteenth came the discovery that he had been tapping the telephone communications of the 62nd Brigade; accordingly, at 9.00 p.m. that night, after a verbal warning of its purpose had been given, a bogus order stating 'operations postponed' was telephoned to companies of the brigade in the front line. It is possible that the ruse succeeded, for there was hardly any hostile machine gun and rifle fire until the British were almost in position: it is certain that the enemy made not the slightest attempt, by patrols or raiding parties, to ascertain if all was normal on his front. When questioned about this want of enterprise, officer prisoners stated that the failure to push out reconnoitring parties was due to there being no reliable NCOs left to lead them, in the German army this was not officers' work.

German records, to the contrary, state that the II/16th Bavarian Regiment in Longueval had been warned to be on the alert and had sent out four patrols, one ran into a British patrol, two returned without discovering anything, the fourth never returned.

The fact that Caterpillar Wood, a major assembly area, was heavily shelled on the night of the 12th /13th but, except for early sporadic shelling, was quiet on the night of the 13th /14th, lends credence to the impression that the enemy was expecting some action on the night of the 12th /13th, but remained unaware of the official postponement.

The assault by the 21st Division, with Bazentin le Petit Wood and the western side of Bazentin le Petit village as objectives, was to be delivered by 110 Brigade (Brigadier-General WF Hessey) together with one additional battalion of 64 Brigade (1/East Yorks) with 98/ Field Company Royal Engineers attached. 62 Brigade (Brigadier-General CG Rawling) held Mametz Wood and 64 Brigade (Brigadier-General HR Headlam) remained in reserve. The brigades were comprised of the following battalions:

110 Brigade 6th 7th 8th & 9/Leicestershire Regiment
                  1/East Yorkshire Regiment (from 64th Infantry Brigade)
                  14/Northumberland Fusiliers (Pioneers)
                  110 Machine Gun Company
                  110 Trench Mortar Battery
                  98/Field Company Royal Engineers

62 Brigade   10/Yorkshire Regiment
12/Northumberland Fusiliers
13/Northumberland Fusiliers
1/Lincolnshire Regiment.

64 Brigade   1/East Yorkshire Regiment (but attached 110th Brigade)
9/King's Own Yorkshire Light Infantry
10/King's Own Yorkshire Light Infantry
15/Durham Light Infantry

The assault brigades of the 7th Division, (Major-General Watts) whose objectives were Bazentin le Grand Wood and then the eastern side of Bazentin le Petit village were:

20 Brigade (Brigadier-General CJ Deverell) to lead, with 95/Field Company Royal Engineers and two companies of 24/Manchester (Pioneers) attached: and 22 Brigade (Brigadier-General JM'C Steele), with 54/Field Company Royal Engineers attached.

In reserve, stationed near Carnoy, south of the old British front line, was 91 Brigade (Brigadier-General JR Minshull-Ford) with 1/3 Durham Field Company Royal Engineers attached.

20 Brigade   2/Border Regiment
8/Devonshire Regiment
2/Gordon Highland Regiment
9/Devonshire Regiment
24/Manchester Regt (Pioneers)
95/Field Company Royal Engineers
20/Machine Gun Company.
20/Trench Mortar Battery

22 Brigade   2/Royal Warwickshire Regiment
2/Royal Irish Regiment
1/Royal Welsh Fusiliers
20/Manchester Regiment.
22/Machine Gun Company.
22/Trench Mortar Battery.
54/Field Company Royal Engineers

91 Brigade   2/Queen's
1/South Staffs
21/Manchesters
22/Manchesters

The attack on the front to the west of the 7th Division was undertaken by the 3rd and 9th Divisions of XIII Corps, to the immediate west of the 7th Division front; 9 and 8 Brigades (3rd Division commanded by

Major General JAL Haldane), and 27 and 26 Brigades (9th Division) completing the assault front to Longueval.

The objectives of 9 Brigade (Brigadier-General HC Potter) included the capture and consolidation of Bazentin le Grand village on the front directly adjoining that of 20 and 22 Brigades.

9 Brigade 12/West Yorks
13/King's (Liverpool)
1/Northumberland Fusiliers
4/Royal Fusiliers
1/1 Cheshire Field Company RE
20/KRRC (Pioneers)
9/Machine Gun Company
9/Stokes Mortar Battery.
56/Field Company RE (assigned to construct fortifications in Bazentin le Grand).

The attention of the German command was diverted from the Bazentin front by other actions taking place nearby on the Somme front during the night of 13/14 July. As diversionary tactics, starting at 2.25 am and continuing until 3.30 am on 14th July, the Fourth Army launched a heavy bombardment on the German line north of the Ancre.

In further operations to capture Ovillers, 3/Worcesters assaulted with parties bombing from the north east, whilst 10/Cheshire and 8/Border attacked from the south-east, and 1/Dorsets from the west.

Trones Wood, on the west flank, was the scene of increasingly desperate action throughout the night of the 13th /14th, eventually being secured at about 9.30 am on the morning of the 15th after fierce, confused, and sustained fighting, during which 6/Northamptons and 12/Middlesex under the command of Lieutenant-Colonel FA Maxwell of the Middlesex Regiment, together with 7/Buffs, sustained very heavy losses. During this engagement, Sgt WE Boulter, 6/Northamptons, performed the deeds which won him the award of the Victoria Cross. His citation reads:

> *For most conspicuous bravery. When a company and part of another were held up in the attack* [on Trones Wood] *by a hostile machine gun, which was causing heavy casualties, Sergeant Boulter, with utter contempt of danger and in spite of being severely wounded in the shoulder, advanced alone over the open under heavy fire in front of the gun, and bombed the gun team from their position. This very gallant act not only saved many casualties, but was of great military value as it materially expedited the operation of clearing the*

Sgt W E Boulter.

enemy out of the wood, and thus covering the flank of the whole attacking force.

(Boulter was born in Wigston, Leicestershire on 14 October 1892 and enlisted in September 1914. He was subsequently commissioned into 7/Northants, and died in 1955.)

110 Brigade was to lead the attack front allotted to the 21st Division adjoining and immediately west of the 7th Division. Its objectives were to capture the German front line and support trenches and the whole of Bazentin le Petit Wood behind, and to link up with 22 Brigade to the north of Bazentin le Petit village.

On 12th July Captain DV Kelly M.C. (later Sir David Kelly, British Ambassador to Moscow), who was 110 Brigade's liaison officer, described his first day in the area:

The Brigade headquarters took over a great German dugout – the first of the kind we had seen – with three stories, beneath the site of Fricourt Chateau. The dug out – which contained hundreds of beds, and had been fitted with electric light – was naturally not forgotten by the German artillery, and I remember the unfortunate carrier pigeons, cage and all, being blown down the entrance staircase. The battalions that same night took over some recently captured German trenches. The next day I visited the lines with Hinkley, the Brigade bombing office. Now for the first time I saw what was to become only too familiar a sight – trenches heaped with dead (mostly, I think, Yorkshiremen), and fields that had become a mere chaos of shell-holes: and now for the first time experienced heavy shell fire. That first day amid the then unfamiliar scenes of slaughter and destruction, pervaded by the equally unfamiliar 'battlefield smell' of churned up earth and rotting corpses, was dream-like in quality, and left but a hazy memory.[6]

On the night of 10th /11th July 110 Brigade relieved 50 and 51 Brigades (17th Division) between Mametz Wood and Contalmaison. They had moved from their positions in the trenches covering Monchy au Bois, just to the north of the active Somme battle, the three day journey being completed by train, bus, and march. They arrived at Dernancourt railhead from there to march to the front, halting at Meaulte to discard by company all but battle order into the battalion quartermasters tent and to collect extra munitions and combat equipment. Dick Read described the scene thus:

...evidences of vast military activities were on every hand: new sidings, camps, huts, wagon and horse lines, lorry parks,

huge dumps of supplies and munitions. Criss-crossing the occasional stretches of arid brown landscape between, were festoons of telephone cables. Amid it all constantly moving ant - like masses of infantry, artillery, horse and mechanical transport, threaded at times by convoys of motor ambulances, each unit in its particular cloud of dust.

After awaking early from a rough sleep in the ruins of Fricourt, he ponders on the scene revealed by the dawn,

the whole terrible story of the 1st July here lay before us like an open book. There were the khaki figures cut down in swathes by the German machine-gunners and hanging on the wire, or on the ground nearby; looking, even in death, as though they were trying to get through it. And then, in the German trench behind, we came on the gruesome sequel. There lay the German corpses, slaughtered by the infuriated remnants of the assailants, who

A typical trench scene experienced by both sides, in this case the trench contains the corpses of Germans.

had seen their mates mown down and at length had won through to get to grips with them. We looked down one dugout steps, now choked with shattered and swollen bodies, two with their machine gun belts around them and their gun and tripod – damaged perhaps by a Mills grenade – on top of them. We could picture them, knocked, shot, or bayonetted into the entrance and the Mills being thrown among them to finish them off. Perhaps, a few yards on, these British lads had met their own fates. We knew now what to expect when our turn came. In those few minutes we seemed to have developed an outlook, half-callous, half-fatalistic. Our feelings of apprehension had gone, had somehow given place to the feeling that, 'up there is the enemy – let's get on with it now and get it over; if we are for it...well, we shall get it'.[7]

9/Leicesters moved up through Fricourt and along Sunshine Alley under continual shelling. Guides from 1/Lincolns had left their trenches to rendezvous with the Leicesters at 4.30 pm – an hour before the remainder of their battalion had attacked and taken Quadrangle Support trench which ran parallel to, and was about 500 yards in front of, the Quadrangle. These two trenches were connected on the left by Pearl Alley, and on the right by Quadrangle Alley.

We eventually got into a trench called the Quadrangle that had been taken the previous day. You can imagine the absolute confusion that exists when a trench has just been taken a few hours previous to relief. We were being shelled extremely heavily all the time, but we had to get to the other trench and relieve it – and so we did. We went over in extended order and lost many of our men. The ground we went over was strewn with dead in every conceivable attitude, both English and German, and the moon was bright, shining down on them, made them look a ghastly sight and made one realise what a terrible thing war is. A little to our right, about a hundred yards from the centre of Quadrangle Support, a large crucifix, with its top blown off, rose up from a small, shell battered cemetery, as if to remind us not to forget Our Saviour, as He had died for us so we might die for our country.

As we could not take over all of the trench, Pearl Alley, which they had been holding, it was left empty, and by doing so one of the first principles of trench warfare were violated, 'holding troops are not to leave until relieving troops are in position'.

After an on the spot discussion between company officers, 9/Leicesters moved to occupy Quadrangle Support and the forward part of Pearl Alley, which was under enfilade fire.

I worked along Pearl Alley, and encountered many terrible sights-English dead were strewn all along the bottom of the trench. When I close my eyes, I can see one sight in particular. It was a poor fellow who must have been blown into the ground, his bare shattered legs cut off just below his hips, were sticking out of the ground. Many times the thought crossed my mind that I myself might be like that any minute – not a pleasant thought.[8]

This forward area was subjected to continual shelling during the day with 105mm shrapnel and 150mm howitzers, resulting in many casualties, and rear area units record at the same time sustained fire from German 120mm batteries.

The deepening and fortification by the Leicesters of the trenches taken over from 1/Lincolns was a top priority.

This was a difficult task, for bombs, ammunition, equipment, and rifles were littered about the trenches and ground above, and on digging down, several bombs were exploded by picks and added to the casualties. As many of the dead as was possible were buried during the darkness, as it was impossible to do this in daylight on account of enemy snipers, who were diligent and accurate. ...The whole country as far as the eye could see was desolate, and sprinkled with dead. Field Artillery batteries, firing 18 pounders, were massed in the open with no cover except brushwood or netting camouflage, almost wheel to wheel, and this but 400 yards from the Front Line. At intervals wagons of the ammunition column dashed up with fresh supplies of shells, dumped them by the side of the guns, and galloped away. Fresh batteries arrived at the gallop, unharnessed, took sights, and commenced firing. Defunct transport and guns lay about in confusion. Enemy shelling was heavy – very heavy at times – and liquid fire was projected onto the front line.[3]

At the time of completion of the relief by the Leicesters at about 4 am on 11 July, the 38th Division had wrested about two thirds of Mametz Wood from the occupying Germans, suffering extremely high casualties in the slow and bloody progress, and were busy consolidating their gains. The northern portion was still controlled by strategically situated German machine-guns, and 22 Brigade was ordered to reconnoitre the situation. Two companies from 2/Warwicks were sent to investigate with a view to capturing the remainder of the wood, the securing of which was becoming an increasingly urgent

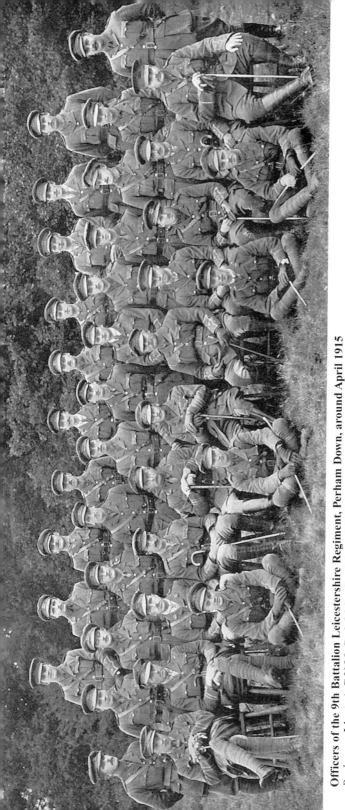

Officers of the 9th Battalion Leicestershire Regiment, Perham Down, around April 1915

Back row: Lieut. A.C.N.M.-P. deLisle, Sec-Lieut. S.T.Hartshorne, Sec-Lieut. P.E.Bent, Sec-Lieut. W.A.Barrand, Sec-Lieut. W.J.Wright, Sec-Lieut. H.J.Barrand, Sec-Lieut. C.E.N.Logan, Sec-Lieut. O.J.Hargraves, Sec-Lieut. G.G.Hargraves, Lieut. A.V.Poyser (RAMC).

Third row: Lieut H.F.C.Anderson, Lieut A.S.Bennett, Sec-Lieut. F.A.Barrett, Sec-Lieut S.W.Sheldon, Sec-Lieut. B de H. Pickard, Sec-Lieut. H.S.Rosen, Sec-Lieut. F.E.Papprill, Sec-Lieut.F.C.Warner, Sec-Lieut. M.L.Hardyman, Sec-Lieut. H.Y.Martin, Lieut .H.E.Milburn, Sec-Lieut A.G.E.Bowell.

Second row: Capt. J.B.Baxter, Major A.W.L.Trotter, Capt. C.R.Dibben, Capt. G.C.I.Hervey, Major J.G.Mignon (2nd in command), Col. H.R.Mead, Major R.B.Unwin, Capt & Adjt. F.N.Harston, Capt. A.E.Boucher, Capt. F.H.Emmet, Lieut. & QM. W.Hunt.

Front row: Lieut. G.E.G.Tooth, Sec-Lieut. A.A.D.Lee, Sec-Lieut. F.Scott, Lieut. H.M.Henwood.

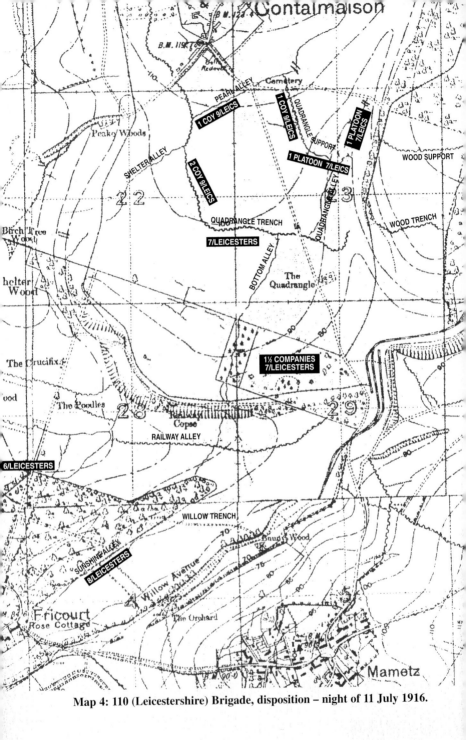

Map 4: 110 (Leicestershire) Brigade, disposition – night of 11 July 1916.

necessity for the successful launch of the Bazentin offensive. 10/Yorkshire (62 Brigade), having received the previous evening a status report from Brigade HQ determining the situation, relieved the 38th Division troops during the night of 11/12 July, completing the relief at 5.30 am. By 9.30 am the whole of the wood was reported as under British control, and 46 German soldiers were under escort to the designated prisoner compound near Fricourt.

The wood received a heavy bombardment of HE and gas shelling throughout the following days but, at the expense of many casualties, the consolidation work continued: 98/Field Engineer Company RE and 14/Northumberland Fusiliers (Pioneers) on fortifications; and 126/Field Company RE on the cutting and construction of access ways and lanes to the sites of forward dumps for use in the forthcoming offensive. 97/Field Company RE and one company of 14/Northumberland Fusiliers, meanwhile, were busy repairing roads and the narrow gauge railway from Bottom Wood to and through Mametz Wood, and a further 300 men of A and B Companies of the 14/Northumberland Fusiliers were engaged in digging cable trenches, and deepening the communication trenches along the edges of the wood.

An impressive array of guns had been captured in the wood; two 8in. howitzers, four 5.9in. howitzers, four 6 in. Siege Guns (taken from Liege), and four 4.2in.howitzers. A multiplicity of chalked up capture credits were claimed; however gained, the final tally remained impressive.

Prior to the attack on Bazentin le Petit Wood Captain Kelly, in his capacity as liaison officer, visited 62 Brigade HQ situated in a German dugout on the western edge of Mametz Wood, and described the spectacle thus:

The wood was everywhere smashed by shell fire and littered

Mametz Wood smashed by shell fire.

Warrant Officers and Sergeants 9/Leicesters, Perham Down July 1915. CSM Robert Hancock 4th from right second row from back.

with dead – a German sniper hung over a branch horribly resembling a scarecrow, but half the trees had had their branches shot away, leaving fantastic jagged stumps like a Dulac picture of some goblin forest. Along the west edge ran a trench, from the side of which in places protruded the arms and legs of carelessly buried men, and as our men moved up that night to attack dozens of them shook hands with these ghastly relics. All the old rides through the wood were blocked by fallen trees and great shell holes, and over all hung the overwhelming smell of corpses, turned-up earth, and lachrymatory gas. The sinister aspect of the wood was intensified that night by the incessant whistling and crashing of shells and the rattle of machine guns and illuminated by the German flares, Very lights, and the flash of bursting shrapnel.[6]

7/Leicesters were detailed to clear and occupy Wood Support Trench, and a company from Quadrangle Trench met with no opposition in fulfilling the order.

From 10 - 13 July 9/Leicesters had recorded 53 casualties including Major AWL Trotter and Second Lieutenant AB Taylor killed, and Second Lieutenant HF King wounded by shellfire, and during the same period 7/Leicesters reported 30 casualties including Second Lieutenant H Spencer, D Company, killed.

Orders were received on 12 July that 110 Brigade would attack Bazentin le Petit Wood on the 13th, and though this was delayed by 24 hours, the relocation arrangements planned for the battalions involved proceeded without change.

A conference held at Brigade HQ on 12 July at 11 am, attended by all commanding officers involved, discussed detailed attack plans, and reconnaissance of the approaches and the assembly areas was undertaken immediately afterwards by commanding officers and staff of the assault battalions.

Further brigade meetings followed on the 13th when it was decided that the barrage on Forest Trench (German second line trench) would lift at zero hour together with that on Flat Iron Trench (German front line trench), not plus one hour as originally intended; but the subsequent lift times were to continue at the intervals as planned.

Due to the lateness of orders being issued, and the consequent lack of time, the original order to use 1/East Yorks to cover the left flank of the attack was changed. Two companies from 8/Leicesters would now undertake this function, and 1/East Yorks would join 9/Leicesters in support of the offensive.

As duty officer on the afternoon of the 12th, Lieutenant de Lisle investigated the left flank of the 9/Leicesters positions and discovered

>...four splendid German dug-outs, about forty feet below ground. I went down into several of them, only to discover they were full of German wounded soldiers. I spoke to several of them, most of whom belonged to the 16th Regiment Bavarian Infantry. They seemed to be in a bad way, till our kind fellows gave them water and food. The British Tommy is a generous fighter, and knows how to treat his prisoners, and gives them food and water, though he may be short himself.

Having arranged that the line be extended to ensure close order with the flanking battalion he returned,

>On my way back I met a Flying Corps officer, who was a particularly nice fellow. He said he had a few hours off. I told him where to find the German prisoners, and that he would find them quite entertaining. This incident shows how the keen fighting spirit of the Royal Flying Corps reveals itself, the officers utilising their spare time to take a survey of the terrestrial battlefield.

>An Artillery Forward Observing Officer was passing by the crucifix (in Contalmaison cemetery) when he saw a dug-out and, going up to see if it was occupied, he found twelve Huns there,

German prisoners being searched before being sent to the rear.

whom he immediately took prisoner and had them sent to the
rear – quite an appetiser!

A and C Companies 9/Leicesters then returned to Quadrangle Trench as positions were exchanged with B and D Companies and, after a proper breakfast and trench kit inspection, the men set to work deepening the trench.

not needing much encouragement in this respect, for the
Bosche shelling was the best incentive.

The sight of the many, many dead and dying of both sides is recalled with horror, soldiers in their trenches being blown apart by shell explosions, and trenches carpeted with bodies. On the evening of 12 July, before 9/Leicesters returned during the night to Fricourt in readiness for the following day's labours carrying ammunition to forward dumps, Lieutenant de Lisle witnessed an aerial encounter:

Four German machines, which we came to the conclusion
were Fokkers, thought fit to carry out a reconnaissance of our
lines. But No! They were to be speedily interrupted by the
appearance of several English machines. Then a great struggle
for the mastery ensued with ever – changing fortune, and the
rattle of the machine – guns became clearly audible. Whenever
the Fokkers thought fit to make a detour over our lines a hail of
anti- aircraft shells, usually termed 'Archibalds' burst all round
them till eventually things got a little too warm for them! Though
no aeroplane was actually brought down, the Germans failed in
their object. This was just as good for us, and it gave them
nothing to report except 'strategic retirement'.[8]

During the night of 12/13 July 10/Kings Own Yorkshire Light Infantry [KOYLI] (64 Brigade), replaced 7/Leicesters in the Quadrangle trenches, the move being completed at 2 am, and troops from 8/Berks (1st Division) relieved 9/Leicesters in Pearl Alley, ready from these positions to effect an attack to capture Pearl Wood. Meanwhile, machine guns, active from strong points established by 98/Field Company RE assisted by a company of 14/Northumberland Fusiliers that same evening along the newly occupied northern edge of Mametz Wood, were effective during the night of the 12th in repelling three separate counter attacks launched from Bazentin le Petit Wood.

The 1st Division, having taken over the newly secured village of Contalmaison from the 23rd Division, west of the forward Leicesters' positions, sent out patrols and found Pearl Wood already evacuated and the road between Contalmaison and Mametz Wood (now the D20) also devoid of enemy troops. 62 Brigade from Mametz Wood established a defensive link along the road with the 1st Division, who themselves established a strongly manned post to secure Pearl Wood.

7/Leicesters and 9/Leicesters withdrew, together with 110/Machine Gun Company and the Trench Mortar Battery, to the old British trenches west of Fricourt, arriving at 5 am on 13 July.

9/Leicesters had little rest before, at 8.30 am, 12 Officers and 600 men fell in in light order – rifle and two bandoliers (100 rounds) – to carry 80,000 Mills bombs forward from Rose Dump in Fricourt to new forward dumps at Mametz Wood in readiness for the following day's offensive. Although supply routes were subjected to repeated shelling, the German built light railway was still useable up to the area of Bottom Wood, where the bombs were off-loaded from the trucks, unpacked, and primed. After repacking the now live bombs into bucket satchels and closing them with tie strings, parties of 50 men – each carrying two bags full – manhandled them to the south east corner of Mametz Wood, where they were handed over to another party for the journey through to the dumps at the north edge. Lieutenant de Lisle commented,

Lt. Alexander de Lisle.

> At a corner of the wood we came across a well constructed German Artillery Observation Post – a tree, with ladders leading up to platforms in three tiers – a good piece of construction.
>
> I met much to my surprise a Lieutenant-General at the bottom north west corner of Mametz Wood. After he had wished me good morning, he asked me what I was doing. I told him and added that I did not consider we should have much difficulty in an attack on the morrow; in fact I thought it would be a walk over. He replied, 'Do not be too optimistic', but I still persisted with as much vigour as a Lieutenant may display to a General.
>
> We lost fairly heavily in accomplishing our purpose but, we told the men, if all the guns in the German army are turned on us, we must still continue to be brave

A German lookout post in Mametz Wood, similar to that described by Lieutenant de Lisle.

Englishmen and men worthy of Leicestershire.

There were a great number of unburied dead; everywhere the whole wood resembled a charnel house. Up both of the outside edges of the wood it seemed that a whole British firing line had been knocked out by some poisonous gas for death had overcome them in their little holes made with their entrenching tools, and in the shell holes. In many cases they still had their rifles up to their shoulders.

After the men of the battalion returned to Fricourt to prepare for the battle, opening before the following dawn, Lieutenant de Lisle with the brigade bombing officer, inspected the dumps, drew maps, completed his report, and made sure no wounded remained unattended, before returning to join his company. The battalion had worked through the day without a break and without lunch.

We managed to get a cup of tea from some privates of the Northumberland Fusiliers who were holding the line on the edge of the wood. It tasted better than anything I had ever had in my life.[8]

6/Leicesters stayed in their positions about Lonely Copse and 8/Leicesters in Sunshine Alley. From near the totally shattered Bottom Wood, fatigue parties carried supplies and ammunition to forward dumps. Dick Read described a scene of shells being brought up:

Happy Valley. I wonder how many men of both sides – and, for that matter how many horses and mules – died along its length during the first fortnight of July 1916. I retain a vivid recollection of our field artillery ammunition columns running the gauntlet to their guns over an exposed portion of road. Approaching the danger spot at the trot with their double teams, then, of a sudden, a mad hell-for-leather ride of five hundred yards or so, the heavily loaded caissons behind jolting and swaying crazily upon the shell-torn track, whilst shrapnel burst around them, with here and there a great black crump of a five-nine in which the team would be lost to view momentarily, to re-appear with the foam flecked and sweating horses rearing madly...but not always.[7]

Green flares, to be used to indicate the front line positions to spotter aeroplanes, were issued, 300 to 110 Brigade, and 200 to 64 Brigade, and picquets were detailed to ensure that Middle Alley, the communications trench running from Mametz Wood into Bazentin le Petit Wood, was used for forward traffic only until the second objective was secured, and thereafter solely for reverse traffic.

Guides would lead the battalions to be on their deployment marks by 3 am, approximately 100 yards outside the northern edge of Mametz Wood, and about 400 yards from the German trench system. 64 Brigade officers and engineers using white canvas tape had stealthily laid out these marks during the previous night.

Whilst the area around Caterpillar Wood was conveniently quiet for the 7th Division preparations, the area about Mametz Wood for the 21st Division was certainly not. From just prior to 3 am the northern part of Mametz Wood in particular was subjected to very heavy enemy bombardment and some machine gun fire, causing numerous casualties amongst the assembled troops before zero hour. The diary of 7/Leicesters records,

> *From 2.55 a.m. when the battalion was assembled on the assault positions, till the barrage lifted at 3.25 a.m., many casualties were suffered from enemy shelling, including half of one of the C Company platoons,* [however] *the men behaved admirably under trying conditions.*

Orders of the day, common to the assault battalions, stated:

> *Every man to carry 2 Mills grenades, 220 rounds of SAA, battalion raiders and platoon grenade groups 20 bombs each, 20 pick and 20 shovels per company, plus green rockets* [for SOS], *and green flares* [for aeroplane signalling from the front line].

Those detailed as grenade carriers would carry two buckets, each containing 18 grenades and 50 rounds of SAA; for those carrying with the attack waves the load was reduced to two buckets of 10 grenades. Provision for water and ration deliveries, as well as bombs, rifle grenades, and Stokes mortar ammunition, to the forward dumps from

The advance water point water carts await filling before transporting their precious loads forward.

the base dump at Rose Cottage, Fricourt, F.4.c.5.6, was a brigade responsibility prior to zero hour. Water was carried forward in petrol cans, more often than not tainted by the original content. After the advance, water wagons would accompany ration wagons to forward dumps, to enable collection by ration carrying parties from the battalions.

After zero hour the division assumed responsibility for moving forward all needed stores to an intermediate dump in Willow Avenue at X.29.b.5.6. Lieutenant Maugham, the Assistant Divisional Grenade Officer, was situated at Rose Cottage Dump, to ensure that all stores and ammunition requisitioned by the brigades through Divisional HQ at Fricourt Chateau were sent forward without delay.

The tramway, which on the 13th extended as far as Bottom Wood, would be restored and extended through Mametz Wood over the following three days, and carry up stores of all kinds. The Advanced Dressing Station was established at Fricourt, and a collecting station at X.29.b.5.6.

At 10.30 pm on the 13th, C and D Companies 8/Leicesters, HQ signallers, and the battalion raiders augmented by additional bombers, started moving up to the battle deployment positions, led by the CO and Adjutant. They left their positions behind Willow trench, thence via the track of the light railway through Mametz Wood. Enemy shellfire persisted throughout the move, inflicting many injuries, and wiping out the C Company Lewis gun team. By 3 am D Company, in two lines of two platoons, were in position with their right on the track of the light railway some 200 yards in front of Mametz Wood, and C Company similarly arranged in platoons at the north edge of the wood. Battalion HQ was established in shell holes in a clearing inside the wood beside the railway track, from where signallers immediately began laying lines back to Brigade HQ. These lines were continually broken by enemy shellfire and field telephone communication was seriously interrupted.

7/Leicesters moved up from their overnight positions in the old British front line trenches behind Fricourt and followed C and D Companies of 8/Leicesters through Willow Avenue and Mametz Wood, to assemble in the four lines of assault, with the forward companies on their marks between the railway and the road about a hundred yards in front of the north east corner of the wood. During the move up

8/Leicesters attack front - 3.25 a.m. 14 July 1916. The German built narrow gauge railway ran alongside the track. The 8/Leicesters attacked to the left - 7/Leicesters to the right.

BAZENTIN-LE-PETIT WOOD

German Front Line

VILLA TRENCH   FLATIRON TRENCH

8/LEICESTERS   7/LEICESTERS

Lieutenant-Colonel Drysdale, 7/Leicesters, was wounded by shell fragments, and the adjutant, Capt A.A.Aldridge, assumed command. (Drysdale was subsequently killed in late Sepember, during the assault on Gueudecourt)

At midnight the supporting A and B Companies of 8/Leicesters left Willow Trench to follow behind 6/Leicesters, who were moving up via the southern and eastern side of Mametz Wood to reach their positions of deployment to the right of 7/Leicesters. Owing to uprooted trees and other debris, only the rear line of 6/Leicesters could be sheltered inside the wood, although the last three lines of the adjoining 7/Leicesters were inside. The supporting A Company of 8/Leicesters lay in the open east of the wood, and the supporting B Company in the north east corner of the wood, awaiting the advance. By 2.55 am, in spite of the shell fire, all the battalions were formed in the four lines of assault formation, on the tapes already laid out.

Dick Read moved with the signallers and runners of 8/Leicesters on the night of 13 July to the forward C Company HQ position in the north of Mametz Wood having attempted, without success, to be drafted back to the Lewis gun section,

> *I remember spending the last few minutes before we started, in having a few words with Freddy Smith and Ted Lineker* [old friends of his with whom much had been shared] *who were busy checking their Lewis ammunition drums. After wishing each other the best of luck and promising ourselves a good booze up when we came out, we parted and took our places in the assembling company.*[7]

The C Company Lewis gun team was subsequently blasted by an explosion; Smith and Lineker never returned, and are commemorated on the Thiepval Memorial to the missing.

9/Leicesters, returned from ammunition carrying duties around 6 pm, and started at midnight the move forward together with the reserve machine guns to the reserve position south east of Mametz Wood. Then, after a brief halt, they continued, to arrive at the north east of the wood at 3.20 am, just as the thunderous opening of the concentrated bombardment roared to its pummelling crescendo.

1/East Yorks (62 Brigade), who had since 5 July been resting and regrouping, absorbing 215 other ranks (117 from 4/East Yorks plus 98 from the Highland Light Infantry and other regiments) as part

Bazentin-le-Petit Wood. Attack front 14 July 1916.

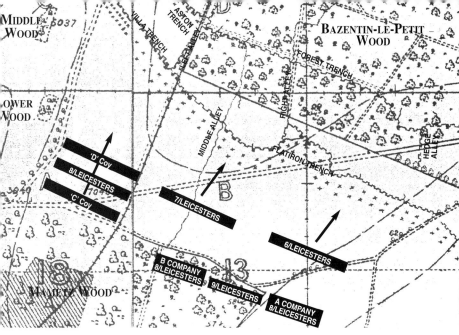

Map 5. 110 Brigade attack formation – 3.00 a.m. 14 July 1916.

replacement for the 441 casualties suffered during the Fricourt fighting from the 1 July, had been seconded to 110 Brigade to support the attack. They had arrived back at Fricourt (Rose Cottage) only at 10.30 pm on 13 July. After a mere two-hour tea break, and having collected grenades and battle equipment, the battalion marched on to the reserve location in the south east of Mametz Wood, and dug in. Although many lachrymatory shells burst in the area, only one casualty was recorded.

The position of the 110 Brigade assault force at 3 am on the morning of 14 July 1916, according to the Divisional Account of Operation was as shown on Map 5.

The Brigade attack formation was to be in six waves,

'A' Wave: 16 Platoons of each of lead battalions in lines of column of platoon at 30 yards distance.

'B' Wave: 4 Platoons of each lead battalion in line with one Stokes mortar per battalion.

'C','D', 'E',&'F' Waves: each 4 Platoons. 8/Leicesters in line in support.

Each wave was to be self contained, each man carrying two bombs, 220 rounds SAA, 2 sandbags, etc. Specific note was made that the clearing in Bazentin le Petit Wood must not be crossed until all the

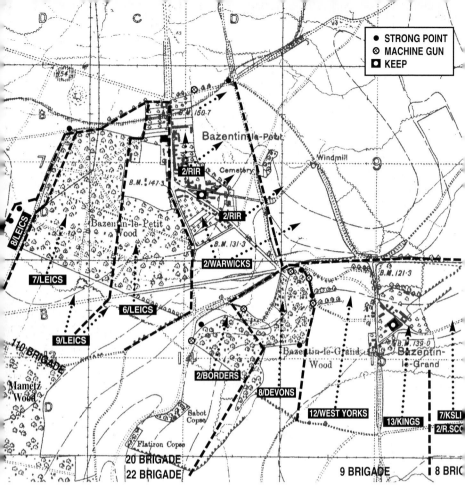

Map 6. Battle of Bazentin Ridge, 14 July 1916. Areas alloted to attack battalions.

buildings in the village to its right were secured.

Rifleman GEM Eyre enlisted in 2/KRRC, proudly known as the 'Black Button Bastards' in August 1914. He was a member of one of a number of bombing parties transferred temporarily from 3 Brigade to augment the bombing resources of 110 Brigade. He and his fellow bombers, whom he named as Rodwell and O'Donnell, reported to the Battalion HQ of 1/Loyal North Lancs Regiment at Scotts Redoubt on 13 July. Led by a sergeant, they traversed the open ground between Mametz Wood and Contalmaison that same evening to join the line between 7/Leicesters and 8/Leicesters, to receive their final briefing in readiness to attack:

> *Our job is to lead the front of the attack and push on into the wood and bomb machine-gun nests till we reach the railway line*

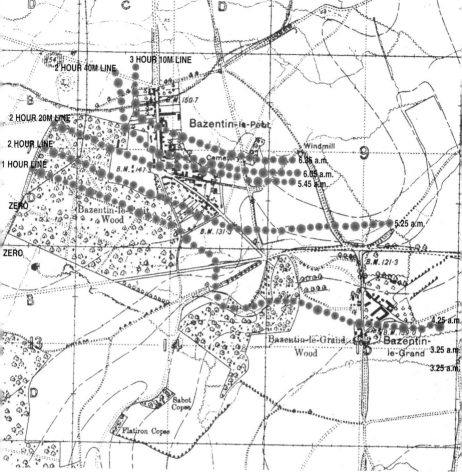

Map 7. The Battle of Bazentin Ridge. Artillery barrage lifts 14 July 1916.

about four hundred yards inside. We will dig in there, and when the following battalions straddle over us, our task is done and we shall withdraw. See that you have plenty of bombs, about twelve each man. Some Leicesters are detailed to follow up with more boxes. We must do our best, as the success of the move lies in scuppering the Hun machine-guns. When Zero goes, men, you go forward, and the Lewis gun will follow you for covering fire.

Moving into the scant forward trench the raiding parties were spaced down the line

We three, a lance corporal from the Sussex, and the officer together, the sergeant and four other men farther off, and another group under a corporal farther away still.[10]

110 Brigade Orders for the assault battalions were as follows.

At 0 (ZERO) A wave will enter the enemy front line trench, the leading line of

platoons proceeding on to the S. edge of BAZENTIN LE PETIT wood, the remaining two lines consolidating the enemy trench.

B wave will join the first two lines of A wave, the whole proceeding into FOREST TRENCH, the 3rd line of A wave remaining in the enemy first line trench to complete consolidation.

At 0 + 95 C wave will enter the enemy first line trench, and continue to consolidate it – the whole of A & B waves will take up a line along the road running East to West in BAZENTIN LE PETIT wood from S.8.d.1/2.3 to S.7.d.5.7/2.

At 0 + 120 D wave will enter FOREST TRENCH and A & B take up a line from S.7.d.6.9 to the junction of six roads at S.8.c./2.8/2 inclusive, along south side of clearing to BAZENTIN LE PETIT to MARTINPUICH road.

At 0 + 140 E wave will occupy line occupied by A & B at 0 + 120. A & B waves will take up a line running from NW corner of BAZENTIN LE PETIT wood to clearing about S.8.a.4.7.

At 0 + 160 F wave will proceed to line occupied by E wave, where they will deposit their loads and form a support. A & B waves will occupy a line from NE corner of BAZENTIN wood to road junction S.8.c.9/2.7.

At 0 + 190 A & B waves will occupy their final objective.

For 8/Leicesters responsible for the left flank of the attack, the orders were:

At ZERO two platoons will enter enemy first line trench and two platoons the enemy second line trench, and form blocks in LEFT ALLEY, and NW of the junction of LEFT ALLEY and VILLA TRENCH and ASTON TRENCH. Two platoons will enter with each successive wave and will work up west side of BAZENTIN LE PETIT wood keeping in touch with the leading wave. The 8/Leicesters will be responsible for LEFT ALLEY. They will move from MAMETZ WOOD on the west side of the tramway, their right keeping in touch with the left of each successive wave.

When the final objective is occupied they will be disposed as follows – on west side of BAZENTIN WOOD TO THE NW corner at S.7.b.7.4.

62 Brigade.... MAMETZ WOOD.

Brigade H.Q.	in old German dugout
10/Yorkshire	E. flank of Wood and 200 yards of Northern edge.
12/North'd Fus.	Remainder of Northern edge of Wood.
13/North'd Fus.	W. flank of Wood.
1/Lincolns	two companies in support across centre of Wood.
	two companies in WOOD TRENCH.

64 Brigade

Brigade H.Q.	FRICOURT Chateau.
1/E.Yorks......	(Attached 110 Brigade.)
9/K.O.Y.L.I.	BOTTOM WOOD.
10/K.O.Y.L.I.	QUADRANGLE TRENCH.
15/D.L.I	LONELY COPSE

The Official History commented

The assembly of the six assaulting brigades of the XIII and XV Corps had been completed with hardly any losses. Except for the shelling on Mametz Wood, nothing more serious than an occasional field gun shell had interrupted the assembly, the outposts covering the deployment had been untroubled by fire or flares, and no enemy patrols had been evident.

Chapter Three

THE FINAL PREPARATIONS OF THE 7TH DIVISION

20 and 22 Brigades were to attack the front allotted to the 7th Division. 20 Brigade was to launch the assault and capture the German front line and support trenches and then the whole of Bazentin le Grand Wood; and then to secure a defensive line along the northern edge. 22 Brigade was to move up through the 20 Brigade defensive line and capture Bazentin le Petit village and cemetery, link with 110 Brigade (21st Division) on their left and 9 Brigade (3rd Division) on their right.

On 5 July, after the struggles of the first day of the Somme battle and the fierce actions which followed: the advance on Mametz village and the costly and tragic action at Mansell Copse, 20 Brigade was withdrawn to rest and refit. 9/Devons 2/Gordon Highlanders and 2/Borders to Ribemont, and 8/Devons, Brigade H.Q, 20/Machine Gun Company, and the Trench Mortar Battery and Bomb Company to Treux.

On 8 July Brigadier-General Deverell carried out a full inspection, and on 9 July the initial order to attack Bazentin le Grand Wood was received by HQ.

Whilst the troops practised the forthcoming action, senior officers reconnoitred the area: Captain Compton-Smith, with the Brigade signals officer for the best site for Brigade HQ, for which Pommiers Redoubt was recommended and selected, and the Brigadier and Staff

A German trench system in a wood, as they wait for the British assault on their positions.

with Lieutenant-Colonel Stanley Clarke, the areas of Caterpillar Trench and the approaches to Bazentin le Grand Wood.

On the morning of 11 July the Brigadier, Brigade Major and the commanding officers of all the battalions involved travelled to XV Corps HQ at Heilly to receive their instructions and to inspect the relief model of the battle area. The commanding officers and battalion officers subsequently reconnoitred the ground approaches to the wood.

Packs were stacked, and in battle order with greatcoats, the brigade moved up to the attack front, 9/Devons in the lead, starting at 1 pm on 11 July. The move was completed during the night of 11th /12th and Brigade HQ established at Pommiers Redoubt.

On 12 July further reconnaissance was carried out ready for an attack on the 13th. A German kite balloon was reported rising to the left of Bazentin le Grand Wood, although neither obvious consequential action nor further sightings followed, and an estimated 600 enemy troops were reported as moving towards Bazentin le Petit from the direction of High Wood. During the night of 12/13 July officers from brigade and the Royal Engineers carefully marked out the forward positions and the access route to them for the assault companies. The job was very stressful. At any time they could have been subjected to artillery fire and were in danger of being discovered and betraying the whole operation. They used 1″ wide white canvas tape delivered from fifty yard long reels, stretched across the whole of the divisional attack front.

In the late morning of the 13th at 20 Brigade HQ a final battle briefing conference assembled. In addition to Brigadier-General Deverell (GOC 20 Brigade) and his staff, and Brigadier-General Steele (GOC 22 Brigade) with staff, attendees included Lieutenant-Colonel Bonham Carter and Captain Hoare from 7th Divisional Staff, and Colonel Head RA, who reported the satisfactory achievement of artillery targets, including wire cutting. During the afternoon the commanding officers of 10 RHA, and 95/Field Company Royal Engineers visited for their final briefings.

20 Brigade Operation Order dated 13 July advised:

> The enemy has been greatly disorganised by our attacks. He has been forced to draw on his reserves from all parts of the front, from the Ypres Salient, from Valenciennes, and from Champagne. These troops have been thrown into the line at the shortest notice.

> The LEHR Regiment (3rd Guards Division) held the line in front of BAZENTIN le GRAND WOOD, with the 122nd Reserve

Troops gather at Minden Post, on their way up to the front line.

Regiment (183rd Division) on its right, and the 16th Bavarian Regiment (10th Bavarian Division) on its left. Numbers of prisoners have been captured from all those units; but so much disorganisation has been caused by the hurried arrival of reinforcements, that it cannot be stated with certainty what units will be met with in, or behind, the German second line.

During the clouded, moonlit night of 13 July the leading assault battalions set off from Minden Post for their final assault positions, with orders to move soundlessly, no loose talk or clanging equipment to betray their movement or to declare their presence. The crashes and rumblings from the continuing bombardment on Mametz Wood a few hundred yards to the west, and the crackle of occasional random fire on their own routes, would no doubt have stifled most noises.

9/Devons, commanded by Lieutenant Colonel HJ Storey, were designated to cover the deployment of the assault battalions and then to follow up the advance. As support troops, the Regimental HQ was established in Montauban Alley near Loop Trench, with No 3 and No 4. Companies towards the eastern end of White Trench and in Montauban Alley, with a platoon at a strong point in Caterpillar Trench, and No 1 and No 2 Companies in the vicinity of Caterpillar Wood, where, having relieved the South Wales Borderers, they were busy digging T-shaped fire trenches on top of the north bank of Caterpillar Valley. With two guns of 20/Machine Gun Corps, one platoon had moved forward to Marlboro Wood. Six machine guns placed in the fire trenches on the high ground of Caterpillar Trench and Montauban Alley were very effective in sweeping the approaches up to the German positions.

Caterpillar Wood was heavily shelled by howitzers and field guns from the direction of Longueval and Caterpillar Trench and the approaches to it were badly damaged. Additional fire of all types of arms from the German lines and from Mametz Wood, the north of which had remained in enemy hands until the morning of 12 July, added to the mayhem.

Patrols were detailed to cover Marlborough Trench - Flatiron Copse - Sabot Copse area during the night of 12/13 July, but most were prevented by the persistent and heavy German artillery barrage. However, one reconnaissance patrol under Lieutenant Costeloe advanced some 600 yards along Marlborough Trench without contact with the enemy. When 8/Devons, who were to lead the assault, moved forward, No 4. Company 9/Devons moved to their assault support position, just north of Caterpillar Wood; No. 3 Company concentrated about the strong point in Caterpillar Trench; and the other Companies remained in Caterpillar Valley.

Up to noon on 14 July, during the moves, 9/Devons suffered 57 casualties: three Officers wounded, four other ranks killed, and 50 other ranks wounded.

2/Borders and 8/Devons were bivouacked at Minden Post awaiting deployment directly to their respective assault positions. Starting at 10.25 pm, on the 13th, Lieutenant Ephraums (Brigade Staff) guided Major James and his 8/Devons in single file via Loop Trench and Caterpillar Trench (meeting en route the Brigade Major on his way to meet with his 3rd Division counterpart at their HQ in The Loop). Broken ground, pitted with fresh craters, haphazard bunches of tangled barbed wire, old trenches needing to be crossed by plank bridges and hostile shelling, all conspired to delay progress, but nevertheless the battalion was in position by 2.35 am, suffering just one casualty during the move, and that an unfortunate accident inflicted by a stray fuse cap from a 6″ shell fired from their own field guns.

The deployment formation, similarly replicated by the other attack groups, was: two companies in half companies forming the front line in column, with the two leading platoons of each company extended at three paces, the other two platoons of each company in the same formation a hundred yards behind, with a further company in support a hundred yards to the rear.

A strong bombing party established a block in Marlborough Trench to cover the deployment, and then moved forward along the trench with the advancing assault troops. These were closely followed by a Stokes mortar section under orders not to open fire unless serious opposition be encountered.

The rest of the trench mortar battery waited with 2/Gordons as reserve. No machine guns were to be taken forward before emplacements covering the final objectives had been established. Two were detailed to cover the advance of 22 Brigade from the north of Bazentin le Grand Wood.

Captain Compton-Smith (Brigade staff) guided Lieutenant-Colonel Thorpe and his 2/Borders, again in single file, via Willow Avenue stream, subjected en route to shelling by field guns firing HE and

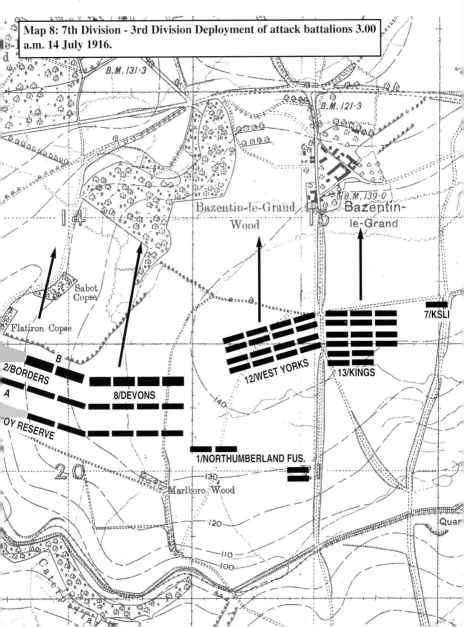

Map 8: 7th Division - 3rd Division Deployment of attack battalions 3.00 a.m. 14 July 1916.

Gordon Highlanders and ammunition limbers moving up – July 1916.

shrapnel then, by the south east of Mametz Wood, along communication trenches and on, following the pre-defined route crossing open, battered ground, littered with old wire and scrap, moving through the two outpost companies of 9/Devons positioned some 200 yards in front of Caterpillar Wood, and assembling in pre-practised formations on the clearly marked assault lines.

The leading companies were behind a slight bank on which young trees were growing, some five hundred yards from the enemy lines (and much closer to the enemy defences on the salient known as The Snout), the flanks bounded on the right by a track marked by a bush of thick low scrub in the direction of Marlborough Wood, and on the left by Flatiron Copse.

The Snout was planned by the Germans to be a heavily fortified salient and construction work had recently been concentrated in the area. Intensive shelling by the guns of the 7th Division heavy trench mortar battery had wrought havoc and the area had been reported by reconnaissance parties as seeming to be unoccupied. Deep dugouts had, in fact, been wrecked and rendered useless by the bombardment and those German soldiers remaining alive had scrambled back to the dubious shelter of the main trench line fronting Bazentin le Grand Wood.

The left of 8/Devons was in contact with 2/Borders some fifty yards west of Marlborough Trench, and, on their immediate right, with 12/West Yorks (3rd Division), who were to attack towards Bazentin le Grand village. When the two assaulting battalions had moved forward to their positions, the rear companies of 9/Devons moved into Caterpillar Valley ready to move up in support as required.

60

2/Gordons, commanded by Lieutenant Colonel Gordon DSO, started from Ribemont at about 2.15 pm on the 11th and, after an hour's rest at Minden Post, moved off again to their assigned position in trenches at Pommiers Redoubt, completing the move at 5 am on the 12th. During the afternoon and evening of the 13th they completed, by platoon groups, the move to their reserve positions in the Hammerhead part of Mametz Wood, where they stayed in readiness. The battalion, in prudently digging six foot deep trenches, avoided serious casualties in spite of enduring a heavy artillery bombardment on the morning of the 14th. The officer commanding was ordered to follow closely the progress of the assaulting battalions and to answer any calls for reinforcement as needed, and immediately.

No.2 Section of 7th Division Signal Company was responsible for the systems of communication. On 11 July a field telephone line was laid to connect 9/Devons with their HQ, and on the 13th the other battalions involved were connected to their respective HQs using a common cable running down East Trench and Montauban Alley. battalion HQs were linked to brigade HQs, and linemen were posted at strategic points ready to repair broken cables without delay. All lines worked well, the main line up to the north end of Caterpillar Wood remained undamaged, and although communications to the forward 8/Devons, 2/Borders and 9/Devons were frequently interrupted,

The Memorial Cross of 2/Gordon Highlanders, Fricourt being viewed by Ben Tullett, August 1916.

efficient reconnections by the alert linemen avoided any serious delays. Visual communications with brigade HQ remained operative throughout the move, and field telephones were installed and intact, although telephone contact with front companies was restricted by order.

20 Company MGC (Machine Gun Corps) was ordered to place eight guns in the line and, after reconnaissance by the commanding officer accompanied by Lieutenants Leck and Drew, and Second Lieutenants Whiteway and Johnson, the best forward positions were determined. No 1 Section was to be in Montauban Alley, with No 2 Section in Caterpillar Trench and a trench off Caterpillar trench to the right about 150 yards forward from Montauban Alley. At 9 pm on 12 July two guns were ordered to Marlborough Wood to help cover the deployments. Lieutenant Leck, with two guns from No.1 Section, held the post until relieved at 6.40 pm on 13 July by Lieutenant Lawley with the other two guns of No.1 Section.

During the nights of 12 and 13 July the six guns remaining on the high ground around Caterpillar Trench swept the enemy wire to deter wiring parties, and fired regular bursts towards the cross roads at the north west of Bazentin le Petit, and at the village itself, much to the annoyance of the occupying German troops.

On 12 July at 9 pm, the Commander Royal Engineers (at Divisional staff) verbally ordered that the 95/Field Company RE wire along the line at Caterpillar Wood but, due to the incessant enemy shellfire, progress on this task was constantly interrupted and finally abandoned about 4 am on the 13th; at which time the section returned to its HQ to report. Much to the relief of the sappers, the situation report having been relayed to Brigade HQ, the GOC was not particularly anxious about the work, and further action was deemed unnecessary. On 13 July the company was kept busy establishing forward dumps in readiness to support the forthcoming offensive, and at 3.25 am on the 14th orders were received to be at muster in Caterpillar Wood by 6.30 am.

24/Manchester Regiment (Pioneers), who were attached to 95/Field Company RE, had been working in the area of Mametz / Minden Post from 1 July before withdrawing for rest and recuperation near Maricourt.

By way of diversion, the Battalion Diary records:

> *8th July 1916. Weather Fine – Regimental sports – Heats morning, semis and finals in afternoon. Prizes presented by the Commanding Officer.*

The battalion returned to full duties and after working about Wellington Redoubt, were ordered forward in readiness for the construction and consolidating work in the Bazentins.

The objectives of 20 Brigade in the attack, as stated in the Operation Order dated 13th July, were as marked on Map 6.

22 Brigade had been in the front line of the Somme battle since 1 July, fighting from the Bois Francais to Fricourt sector, through to Mametz, there being relieved by the 38th Division on the 5th and had withdrawn to Heilly, where the Brigade absorbed replacements for the recent heavy losses, rested, regrouped and reorganized. On 8 July the GOC 7th Division, Major-General HE Watts, addressed the Brigade, and on the 9th orders were received to move up to the Citadel via Plum Lane, in readiness to attack either Mametz Wood or Bazentin. The move was completed by 9.30 pm on the 10th and immediately followed at 11 pm by an order to clear and occupy Mametz Wood. This order, in turn, was rapidly aborted, but not before the four battalions had moved off, the rapid change no doubt causing some choice comments in the ranks as to the suitability of those above to direct such operations. The battalions returned to bivouac: 2/Royal Warwicks and the Machine Gun Company to the Halt, 2/Royal Irish Regiment, 1/Royal Welsh Fusiliers, and 20/Manchesters to the Citadel.

Warned by Divisional HQ at 8.20 am on 11 July, an order was received at 7.30 pm by Brigade HQ to ascertain the situation in Mametz Wood, and then to complete its occupation. Immediately upon receiving the order a reconnaissance party, consisting of A & B companies of 2/Warwicks, lead by Captain Wasey, left to investigate. After an on the spot consultation with Brigadier-General Evans, commanding 115 Brigade in the wood, the party scouted and reported the north edge of Mametz Wood still to be in German occupation, and that enemy machine guns effectively guarded the edges and the rides - the only way through the damaged, densely tangled, and virtually impassable northern part of the wood. During this operation Second Lieutenant JAK Gildea and two other ranks were killed, 13 wounded and 4 posted as missing. Captain Wasey, after reporting to Brigadier-General Evans (115 Brigade were at the time awaiting the arrival of relieving infantry for the 38th Division) returned with his troops, to bivouac at the Halt, arriving at 1.30 am on the 12th and awaited further orders. Divisional HQ was advised at noon on 12 July that Mametz Wood had been cleared of enemy troops and no further action by the brigade was necessary. In fact, some pockets of resistance remained in the northern fringes, but by that evening all opposition had been finally removed or had withdrawn.

On the 13th, at 3.40 am, orders were received confirming the delayed attack plans on the German second line and 22 Brigade HQ was established in White Trench. 2/Warwicks, and 2/Royal Irish Regiment (RIR) were assembled south east of Mametz Wood, ready to move up, in support; 1/Royal Welsh Fusiliers (RWF) camped in White Trench, and 20/Manchesters in reserve in Fritz Trench.

The disposition of the assault Brigades at 3 am on the morning of 14 July 1916, was as follows:

20 Brigade in position ready to lead attack.

Brigade H.Q.	MONTAUBAN ALLEY.
2/Borders	with left in the valley 100 yards west of FLATIRON COPSE, and with right in contact with 8/Devons at S.20.b.1.9.
8/Devons	with left in touch with 2/Borders and east to the track S.20.b.8.8.in contact with 3rd Division.
2/Gordons	MAMETZ WOOD
9/Devons	CATERPILLAR WOOD with a detachment at Marlborough Wood.
20/Company MGC.	MONTAUBAN ALLEY and CATERPILLAR WOOD with a detachment with 9/Devons at Marlborough Wood

22 Brigade

Brigade H.Q.	WHITE TRENCH
2/Warwicks	MAMETZ WOOD
2/R.I.R.	MAMETZ WOOD
1/R.W.F.	WHITE TRENCH
20/Manchesters	FRITZ TRENCH
22/MGC.	MAMETZ WOOD

91 Brigade in reserve about CARNOY.

2/Queen's
1/South Staffs
21/Manchesters
22Manchesters.

The preparation and deployment had been an unqualified success. All was set for the intensified pre-assault bombardment, and zero hour of The Battle of Bazentin Ridge.

Chapter Four

THE PREPARATION OF THE 3RD DIVISION

The right flank of the Battle of Bazentin Ridge was directed by XIII Corps, using 9, 8, and 76 Brigades. The actions of 8 Brigade and 76 Brigade against Longueval are covered in detail in companion books in the Battleground Europe series (Delville Wood and High Wood), and are only briefly mentioned in this volume.

The assault on the German positions in the sector of the front between Bazentin le Grand Wood and Waterlot Farm, was assigned to the 3rd Division, 9 Brigade covering a front of 800 yards, against Bazentin le Grand Village on the left, and 8 Brigade against the front to Longueval on the right.

9 Brigade (GOC: Brigadier General HC Potter) comprised:
> 12/West Yorks
> 13/King's Liverpool
> 1/Northumberland Fusiliers
> 4/Royal Fusiliers
> 56/Field Company RE
> 1½ Companies 20/KRRC (Pioneers)
> 1 Section 1/1 Cheshire Field Company RE

8 Brigade, (GOC: Brigadier General EG Williams) comprised:
> 8/East Yorks
> 7/Shropshire L.I.
> 1/Royal Scots Fusiliers
> 2/Royal Scots
> 1 Company 20/KRRC (Pioneers)
> 1 Section 1/1/Cheshire Field Company RE.

To the right of the attack by the 7th Division, the assaulting battalions of 9 Brigade were: 12/West Yorks on the left, and on the right 13/King's Liverpool, whose objectives included the capture of the village of Bazentin le Grand.

1/Northumberland Fusiliers were in brigade reserve and 4/Royal Fusiliers held in divisional reserve. 9/MGC allocated four guns to 13/King's, and two guns to 12/West Yorks, with four guns operating indirect fire on the valley north of Bazentin le Grand village and wood until zero hour, and two guns remaining in divisional reserve stationed at Caterpillar Wood. Each assaulting battalion was allotted two trench mortars, with another four in reserve with the 1/Northumberland Fusiliers.

After the fighting of the first days of the Somme Battle, 9 Brigade had spent some time in the vicinity of Carnoy whilst the battalions reorganised and regrouped. The days immediately prior to the Bazentin action were spent in establishing forward dumps and reconnoitring the ground to be attacked, and by night, between the hours of 10.30 pm and 2.00 am, whilst shelling was halted, inspecting (and cutting where necessary) enemy barbed wire defences, and practising battle formation and assembly in the darkness.

Similarly to the other assault brigades, the quantities of supplies to be carried up during the two days before zero, in this case from 3rd Divisional Dump, to be stored at the brigade dump near Loop Trench, were specified as

> 5000 Grenades.
> 64 boxes Lewis gun ammunition.
> 48 boxes Machine gun ammunition.
> 256 boxes Rifle ammunition.
> 1400 Rations.
> 330 Tins of water.
> 1600 Trench mortar bombs.

Forward half battalion dumps situated in Caterpillar Valley were to be stocked with:

60 Picks	50 Screw Stakes long
60 Shovels	50 Angle Iron Stakes long
3000 Sandbags	10 Mauls

20 Coils French Wire	4 Felling Axes
20 Coils Barbed Wire	5 Bill Hooks
50 Wooden Stakes – long	3 Handsaws
100 Wooden Stakes – short	1 Cross cut Saw.
2000 rounds for Lewis guns	500 Grenades
4000 rounds for Machine guns	
64 boxes x 100 rounds Rifle ammunition.	

On 12 July Brigade HQ was relocated in The Loop, and on the 13th final preparations were completed. One officer and thirty men from each unit, to include those not considered fit for the fighting line, were detailed to bring forward SAA, bombs, picks and shovels, tins of water, barbed wire coils, etc., from the forward dumps to the front line as the battle progressed.

The Orders for Officers in Charge of Dumps issued by 9 Brigade, similar to those issued by the other brigades involved, illustrate the meticulous detail with which the battle and in particular the logistics were planned and are quoted as follows in their entirety.

1. You are in charge of the Dump and a party detailed for carrying

2. All dump Officers with their parties will rendezvous near the Brigade issuing dump near LOOP trench at an hour and on a date to be notified later, and will move under Captain COOPER via the Brigade marked route to their dumps in CATERPILLAR valley, probably being the last unit in the Column.

3. On arrival at their respective dumps, each party will commence carrying material forward from their dumps up the Road indicated on the night 12th/13th. Two forward dumps about 500 Yards up this road and on each side of it but well clear, will be formed. - Material from A and B Dumps to Right dump, that from C and D Dumps to Left dump. - Trench Mortar Ammunition only will be carried forward from the Brigade dumps. - From the half Battalion dumps, the following is to be carried forward;-

     5 Boxes S.A.A.
     4 Rolls Barbed Wire
     5 Rolls French Wire
     10 Screw Stakes
     1 Maul
     10 Long Pickets
     20 Short Pickets.

From the Brigade Dump.-

     160 Stokes Bombs. (one journey of 40 men)

This Stokes Ammunition will be divided equally between the two dumps.

4. Having completed the carrying to the four dumps, A and B dump will leave 8 men each with B dump Officer in charge at Right forward dump. C and D dump will leave 8 men each with D dump officer in charge at Left forward dump. All the remainder will return to their original dumps.

A and B dumps coming under charge of A dump Officer.

C and D dumps coming under charge of C dump Officer.

Messages will reach dump Officers during the Operations for material by runner. It is the duty of the carrying parties to at once carry forward to the captured *position the material etc required, the carrying parties returning to their dumps on dumping their material. No rations or water will be issued from the Brigade dump without an order from the Brigade H.Q. to do so. It will be the duty of A, B, C and D dumps to fill up the two forward dumps as they become depleted. Depletion in A, B, C and D dumps should be reported to Brigade H.Q. through Advanced Report Centre from time to time.*

K.A.Buchanan
Major
Bde Major. 9th Infy. Bde.

The brigade advanced report centre was to be established in a dug out in the communications trench south of Marlborough Wood. Each battalion would run a cable forwards from this point to enable a field telephone link to be established, and signals by sheets, mirrors, and flares, to indicate positions, would be communicated to reconnaissance aeroplanes, recognisable by having a black band painted on the underside, and trailing streamers. Green flares were to be burnt on reaching the German support line, and again on securing the road running east to west beyond the north end of Bazentin le Grand, red and yellow flags were to be waved to indicate to the artillery the most advanced infantry positions, and yellow flags waved by bombing parties working along trenches to signal their position. Visual signalling connection was also established, and each battalion appointed runners to convey messages to and from battalion and brigade headquarters.

Coloured material was issued to make bands to be secured under the shoulder straps of the soldiers involved. The infantry were identified by company: A & W – blue; B & X – green; C & Y – red; D & Z – yellow; those carrying wire cutters were to tie a white tape round the right shoulder strap, and those in working parties attached to the Royal Engineers white tape around both shoulder straps.

Great emphasis was placed in divisional instructions that all involved must be well trained and briefed in detail as to their specific tasks, and that carrying and working parties were of equal importance, and were expected to complete their duties with even more determination and dedication than those directly engaged in the assaults.

Paragraph 16 of the preliminary attack instructions issued by Major KA Buchanan, the Brigade Major of 9 Brigade, states:

Troops will advance to within charging distance in quick time.
The assault will be delivered without cheering.

During the night of the 13th the assault battalions moved forward and by 1.45 am were in the deployment positions specified in attack orders,

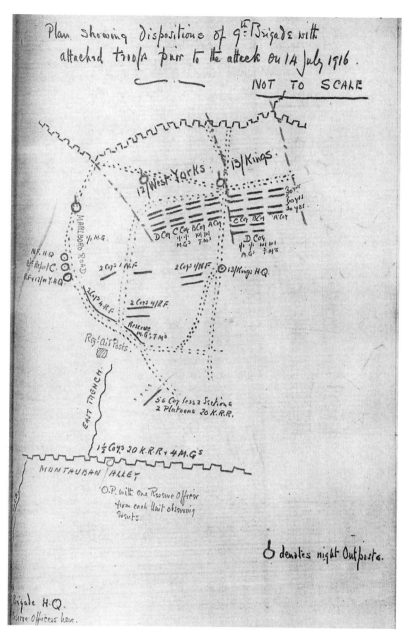

Plan showing dispositions of 9th Brigade with attached troops prior to the attack on 14 July 1916.

NOT TO SCALE

12/West Yorks from the east end of Caterpillar Wood to Marlborough Wood, and 13/King's from the east of Caterpillar Wood westwards to where the light railway track crossed the Montauban to Bazentin road. When these assault battalions moved forwards to their attack positions they were replaced by 1/Northumberland Fusiliers and one section of

1/Cheshire Company RE, in readiness for their move forward in support. By 3.00 am on 14 July the assault battalions had formed, without casualties on the lines marked out by Brigade officers during the previous night, and were positioned ready to spring the attack, with their first objective, the German front line trench some one hundred and fifty yards ahead.

The Battalion War diary noted that three Prussian soldiers had been taken prisoner by troops of 12/West Yorks after a small skirmish with an outpost patrol on the night of 13/14 July, but the presence of the massed army was not betrayed by the incident, and remained undetected. The prisoners, when interrogated, said that no immediate action was suspected by troops in the German trenches, however German war records state that at 2 am a sentry of the I/16th Bavarian Regiment had reported British troops in close proximity to the wire in front of Bazentin le Grand, and that as result the battalion in the village was stood to arms.

The ebb and flow of closely fought battles is fraught with complication at the best of times and under the most bland of conditions. Dissemination of the records of actions which took place in damaged and war torn wooded areas is difficult, and in built up areas, however small, the tracking of close combat engagement is rendered open to differing interpretation. Cataloguing the progress of an intensely fought battle such as this, on a narrow front, lasting a short period of time, but encompassing both wood and village, sometimes becomes clouded in confusion. Contradictory timings, dubious map references, duplicated and exaggerated claims to glory and inferred denials of responsibility, the pride of regiments and commanders at all levels, complicate the search for what actually happened. All of these factors combine with delays in registering details of the action, in many cases inevitably using second hand information, and result in a degree of detection and subjective probability being applied to determine, and to record, as true an account as is possible of the battle as it unfolded.

The variations on the recurrent hells of the Somme battles continued their bloody progression. The battle this day, albeit judged militarily a great success, was amongst the vilest, and the courage and bravery of all the men and their leaders involved in the fighting is beyond doubt. Critical situations arose calling for extraordinary and unflinching determination by attackers and defenders alike. Successive incidents throughout the day, involving exhausted individuals, against a background of killing, maiming, and the stench of death, highlighted the hatreds of close combat, and of contradictory kinships, fused together by the shared experience in the murderous bedlam which ruled the day.

The recorded action is presented by Division, but as the battle proceeded boundaries became blurred, brigade fronts became less defined, and battalions intermixed.

Chapter Five

3rd DIVISION: THE ATTACK OF THE 14 JULY AND THE FOLLOWING DAYS

The Official History (somewhat contradicted by records of the morning dead in battalion diaries) states:

At 3.20 am the whole sky behind the waiting infantry of the four attacking divisions seemed to open with a great roar of flame. For five minutes the ground in front was alive with bursting shells, whilst the machine guns, firing on lines laid out just before dark the previous evening, pumped streams of bullets to clear the way. When the barrage lifted at 3.25 a.m. the leading companies rose and advanced through the ground mist at a steady pace. There was just enough light to distinguish friend from foe. Surprised by the shortness of the intensive and most effective bombardment, by the deployment of the stormers so near in the dark, and by the creeping barrage of high explosive, the enemy made but a feeble and spasmodic resistance to the first onslaught

The leading British wave reached the German wire before a shot was fired, and in the hostile trenches the only serious opposition came from men who rushed from dug-outs and shelters after the first wave had passed to engage those which followed. The enemy counter-barrage, when it came down a little later, fell in Caterpillar Valley, behind the assaulting troops.

At 3.20 am the intense bombardment concentrated along the whole front, and the forward troops crept to within a few yards of the German

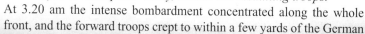

first trench, awaiting the 3.25 am lift. Rising and hurriedly advancing, on reaching the crest of the rising ground, 13/King's were raked by machine gun fire from the front trench and housetops in Bazentin le Grand village, but the wire here had been well cut, and the attacking troops quickly overpowered the few occupants remaining in the front trench, who offered little resistance at close quarters. Then, without delay, they pressed onwards to occupy the second line trench, but came under withering rifle and machine gun fire from both the village and the communications trench on their right flank.

The line of the second trench directly fronting Bazentin le Grand was hardly detectable, having been pulverised by the barrage, and multiple casualties were incurred by 13/King's as, in the confusion of battle, many of the attackers, pinned down by the concentrated fire, withdrew into the damaged front trench. A battered but recognisable stretch of the second line trench adjoining the road was occupied, whilst a considerable number continued forward into Bazentin le Grand village to suffer from the artillery barrage, which did not lift from the 'one hour line' there until 4.25 am.

The depleted ranks of 13/King's advanced through the village as soon as the barrage lifted, B Company on the left of the road, D Company on the road, and C Company on the right of the road. They entered the village by skirting to the left of the Keep. Continual sniping and sudden bursts of machine gun fire from the ruined buildings made the progress slow and extremely hazardous. Second Lieutenant Clark and his carrying party managed to get through with a substantial quantity of bombs, enabling an immediate improvement in progress by the restocked bombing parties. On the extreme right, A Company suffered sudden and severe casualties when exposed to rifle grenade and bomb attack from a German occupied communication trench that had not yet been reached by the delayed 8 Brigade troops. They were soon augmented by the Stokes mortars and bombers of 1/Northumberland Fusiliers and the German assailants were forced to withdraw. Lieutenant Sellars, the signalling officer, earned particular mention at this time for his work in the village, under constant fire, whilst establishing telephone links between the battalion and forward HQs.

12/West Yorks, advancing between 13/King's and 8/Devons of the 7th Division on their left, had also been unable to locate any semblance of the first and second line German trenches, so battered were they by the barrage, and many overran into the continuing artillery bombardment. The strength of the remainder, hurriedly digging in where the battered line was thought to be, was rapidly depleted by machine gun fire from both Bazentin le Grand village and wood, which persisted until the flanking forces had progressed. The machine guns allotted to the Battalion were speedily called upon to rake the German positions in front of the village, and an urgent call for reinforcements was timed at 4.39 am. Patrols were sent forward and a strongpoint with two Lewis guns and a machine gun was set up at S.15.a.3.8 on the track running alongside Bazentin le Grand Wood. Strong points were to be constructed by 12/West Yorks and Cheshire Company RE on the old German first line trench at S.15.c.5.7 and S.15.c.2.4, although these were not completed. During the action Captain CR Sharp and Lieutenant AG Scarr were killed and subsequently recommended for decoration, as were Captain Sir AE Dunbar, Lt EC Squires, and Captain HS Sugars RAMC.

Meanwhile, the wounded Lieutenant Colonel AStH Gibbons, Commanding 13/King's, who had already lost most of his officers, and with his remaining forces scattered in the village, had also requested urgent assistance, timed in brigade records at 5.11 am.

Both calls were answered by 1/Northumberland Fusiliers, who had quickly vacated their reserve positions in the sunken road, some 250 yards south of the village. They were immediately replaced there by three companies of 4/Royal Fusiliers moving up from Marlborough Trench, and 56/Field Company RE with one and a half companies of 20/KRRC (Pioneers) moving up the Montauban – Bazentin Road. Half a company of 4/Royal Fusiliers, under direction from 1/Cheshire

Map 9: 1/Northumberland Fusiliers move to support the assault battalions 5.00 am 14 July 1916.

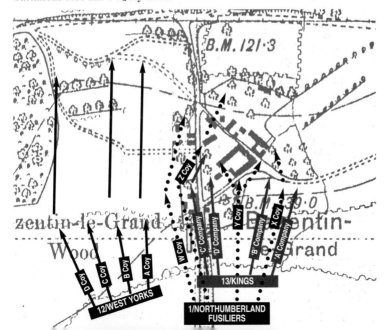

Company RE, immediately began digging a communications trench back from the captured German front line southwards to the base of the ridge.

Just after 4 am the advance (Y) Company of 1/Northumberland Fusiliers had moved forward by platoon to lead the supporting forces, and had deployed along the newly won trenches. At about 5 am, Lieutenant Colonel Gibbons, who was subsequently again injured and found lying mortally wounded and under fire in open ground to the left of the road, requested Lieutenant CM Cooper, 1/Northumberlands, who with a platoon of Y Company had pushed forward, to assume command of the remaining 13/King's. Lieutenant Cooper with his platoon moved towards the village, soon to be joined there by two further platoons of Y Company, the Stokes mortars, X Company under Captain Routledge, Z Company under Captain White to guard the left flank, and part of W Company. This latter company, under the command of Lieutenant Taylor, had opportunely stormed forward to

Plan of the Keep and fortifications, Bazentin Le Grand.

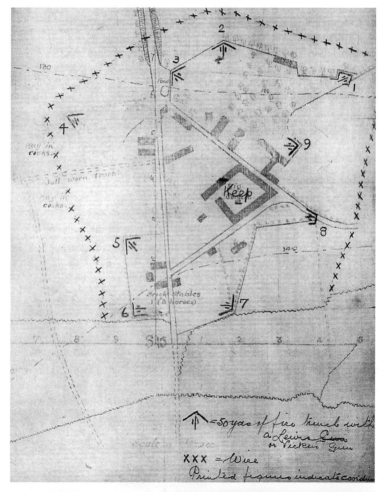

Before the onslaught. Farm buildings – Bazentin le Grand – June 1916.

fill a gap which had opened between 13/King's and 12/West Yorks to the left of the road soon after zero hour, and had captured and consolidated there a stretch of the front and second line trenches.

The lead company of 1/Northumberlands met with considerable machine gun and sniper fire from the site of the Keep on the east side of the village and suffered multiple casualties before successful bombing silenced the guns, and forced twenty Germans, including the HQ Staff of the 10 Bavarian Regiment, to surrender from the large cellar. Owing to the smashed condition of the buildings, a thorough search, especially of the cellars, proved to be extremely difficult, sniping was rife, and death and injury by rifle fire sudden and frequent.

Lieutenant Lynch, with a party of X Company bombers, stormed a strong enclosure in the large farm on the right of the village, and many were killed, but with great bravery and determination the positions were wrested from the defenders, about twenty prisoners taken, four destructive machine gun posts disabled, the gunners killed, and the guns captured.

Fierce house to house fighting eventually forced the village defenders to take refuge in the rough ground to the immediate north east of the village. Just after 7 am a patrol of 1/Northumberlands probing forward from the village towards Crucifix Corner came under heavy flank fire from German machine guns relocated in the gully running east to west, which contained strongly constructed dugouts. An attempt to rush the positions left many dead on both sides, and the Stokes mortars were summoned forward.

The village of Bazentin le Grand was finally cleared of German troops around 9.30 am but, 8 Brigade had been held up by uncut wire and had had to clear the German trenches by bombing inwards from the flanks, delaying their progress, and leaving the ground directly east of the village unsecured.

An eastwards patrol of 2/Warwicks from the north of Bazentin le Grand Wood, on reaching Crucifix Corner and discovering many bodies freshly dead, alerted 1/Northumberland Fusiliers by runner as to their presence, and shortly after added their firepower to X Company, together with bombers lead by Second Lieutenant Carrick and the Stokes mortar battery commanded by Captain Holmes, and forced the German soldiers out. About seventy surrendered, and many more, forced to flee in a north easterly direction up the valley towards High Wood, became easy targets, and were cut down by fire from the Lewis gun just installed in the village and the added concentrated rifle fire from engineers and pioneers working on the construction of the fortifications.

56/Field Company RE with one and a half companies of 20/KRRC as pioneers worked on constructing a Keep in the village, enclosing the whole area with barbed wire, and completing the fortification with nine fire trenches each with machine gun emplacements.

The work on the Keep and the defences on the west side continued without interruption during the action in the north east, but work on the east side defences could not start until German troops were finally cleared from the area, just before 10 am.

Later in the morning an RFC reconnaissance aeroplane dropped a report that German troops were assembling in numbers north of High Wood, but the subsequent counter attack was directed against positions north and east of Bazentin le Petit and, although subjected to shell fire throughout the afternoon, no infantry action bothered the 9 Brigade front.

As soon as the village and surrounding area was secured, the depleted 13/King's were withdrawn to the now consolidated line of the German front trench, where they remained under heavy bombardment until retiring to Talus Wood to bivouac. Three companies of 1/Northumberland

Relief after the battle. Derelict Hanson Cab – Bazentin Le Grand – July 1916.

Fusiliers remained to defend the area up to and including the Contalmaison – Longueval road, along which, with 12/West Yorks, they established a defensive line of strong posts. Major WD Oswald DSO, the Commanding Officer 12/West Yorks, was mortally wounded by a shell fragment during the evening of the 14th. His battalion remained in position until relieved by 2/Warwicks on the night of 19 July.

The advanced dressing station was situated in the quarry just east of the Montauban – Bazentin road at S.22.c.0.5. The Brigade HQ moved to dugouts adjacent to this road in Caterpillar valley during the evening of 14 July, remaining until 9 Brigade was relieved by 23 Brigade on 19 July and withdrawn to bivouac at Talus Wood. The brigade returned to fight again at Longueval and Delville Wood.

The recorded losses by the Brigade on 14 July 1916 were:

	Officers			Other ranks			
(Killed/Wounded/Missing)	K	W	M	K	W	M	Total
1/Northumberlands	-	4	-	23	148	40	215
4/Royal Fusiliers	-	5	-	7	32	2	46
13/King's Liverpool	8	9	1	117	243	61	439
12/West Yorks	7	7	-	74	235	19	342
9/MGC	2	2	-	2	5	1	12
9/TM Battery	-	-	-	1	8	-	9
Total	**17**	**27**	**1**	**224**	**671**	**123**	**1063**

9 Brigade registered the capture of 70 Prisoners, four field howitzers and six machine guns on this day.

'Using the line'. Wounded being transported 14 July 1916. Probably 7th Division troops heading for the Advance Dressing Station at Mountauban Quarry – now the site of Quarry Cemetery.

Chapter Six

THE ATTACK OF 7TH DIVISION: 14 JULY 1916

At 2.55 am, as the artillery continued its bombardment, the leading platoons of the assaulting companies in the 7th Division sector began to crawl forward. By 3.20 am they were some 50 yards from the German front line, and by the time the intense barrage lifted at 3.25 am they were in many places only 25 yards distant, with the deafening blast, smoke and flames of intense shell bursts just ahead of them. They entered the trenches almost as the barrage ended, much to the surprise of the German infantrymen huddled within, who offered, with few exceptions, only token resistance. Some of the casualties suffered by the assault troops at this stage were inevitably caused by their too daring an approach to the barrage curtain, and some from their own short falling artillery shells. Many of the Germans remained in dug outs, and when refusing calls to surrender (where calls were made), and where hostile rifle fire was encountered, were bombed.

Both forward and second trench lines had been severely battered by the bombardment, and many dead German soldiers lay around either killed in their positions by the inescapable eruption of the ground under the fierce onslaught of high explosives, or blasted by the bombardment whilst attempting to escape back towards the illusory shelter of Bazentin le Grand Wood. Several prisoners were taken from the front trenches, and many more in the wood.

An aerial view of Bazentin Le Grand wood showing the line of the German front trench and The Snout.

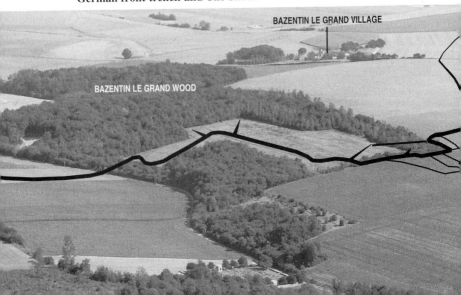

BAZENTIN LE GRAND VILLAGE

BAZENTIN LE GRAND WOOD

German soldiers killed in their positions by the fierce onslaught of high explosives.

The original artillery bombardment plan was that the second line support trenches would be the 'one hour line' This was subsequently re-timed (no easy task), the barrage lifting off the German first and second lines together, and the original 'one hour thirty five minute' line became the 'one hour line'.

At 3.20 am Captain Compton-Smith (Brigade staff) had reported 2/Borders and 8/Devons were in position, the dividing line between the battalions being Snout Trench, which continued into Marlborough Trench. The disposition of 2/Borders in their assault positions was: On the left D Company, under Captain A Wright, and on the right B Company, under Captain RF Newdigate with both companies forming the first and second lines with two platoons in each line. The third line, in line of platoons, was A Company, under Captain PR Dowding. C Company under Second Lieutenant EL Holland formed the fourth (reserve) line, with two platoons at Flatiron Copse, and two platoons in Caterpillar Wood with Lieutenant Colonel Thorpe and his Battalion HQ.

The disposition of 8/Devons under the command of Major BC James, on the right of 2/Borders was:

Two companies in half companies forming first and second lines, a hundred yards apart. The third company formed a support line a further one hundred and fifty yards behind, with a fourth company in reserve. The left connected with 2/Borders at S.20.b.1.9 and the right with 12/West Yorks (3rd Division) at S.20.b.8.8. The Battalion HQ was located in Marlborough Trench at S.20.d.5.9.

The Company HQ of 20/Machine Gun Corps was established at the junction of Caterpillar Trench and Montauban Alley, from where an established telephone link to Brigade HQ was available. Messages to the forward guns were conveyed by runners.

After survey and conferences at Brigade HQ the following positions were selected for gun sites.

(1) Two guns at S.14.b.10.20 to fire north east along valley. (Lt Whiteway No4 Section)

(2) Two guns at S.15.a.10.80 to fire along Bazentin le Petit road and the road running west. (Lt Lawley No 1 Section)

(3) Two guns at S.15.a.30.80 to fire North West and North. (Lt Drew No 3 Section)

The two guns on station in Marlborough Wood to cover the deployment of the forward assault troops remained in that position until moving forward to position (2) above. Six guns were manned in the trenches above Caterpillar Wood, spraying the German wire and Bazentin le Petit village. 20/Company MGC report stated:

It was found during operations on the First of July that after giving covering fire and firing off thousands of rounds, the guns engaged required to be thoroughly overhauled. It was decided therefore that the guns to move forward should not be used for covering fire.

Two guns of each section remained in reserve, plus No 2 Section with its four guns. As Caterpillar Wood was being heavily shelled, to avoid damage, all remaining guns were retained in the vicinity of Company HQ.

At three minutes before the 3.25 am zero hour, the four guns of No 2. Section lifted to 2,800 yards and for 35 minutes concentrated a 10000 round machine gun barrage, covering in wide sweeps the area from S.8.c.10.90 to S.9.d.90.50. The two guns of No.1 Section maintained fire at the German front line until zero hour.

The guns of 20/Company MGC would remain at their stations throughout the day until 9 pm, when Lt Whiteway and his guns, were relieved by Lt Lang and the other two guns of No 4 Section, and Lieutenant Drews and his guns moved forward to the cemetery. The other two guns of No.3 Section took over at position (3) on the west

The view from Flatiron Copse to Bazentin Le Petit. The attack front of D Company 2/Borders .

side of Bazentin le Grand Wood just south of the road.

8/Devons and 2/Borders leading the assault on Bazentin le Grand Wood from their positions behind the bank, in the half light of early dawn, found only bodies of the dead in the area of the Snout salient, and pressed on to find the enemy first line wire and trenches almost completely destroyed.

The right attacking company of 8/Devons cleared the front line trench without much opposition, bombed dugouts and entered the second line at 3.45 am. Patrols were pushed out into the north east of the wood towards the 'one hour' barrage line, and these captured and sent back about 60 prisoners, who surrendered without undue resistance.

Strong points were established at S.15.a.40.65, and S.15.a.1.2 (on the south east and east edges of the wood), but many casualties resulted when the area came under very heavy shellfire which rained down on Bazentin le Grand Wood between 4.30 and 5.30 am.

The Lewis machine gunners firing from the strong point on the higher ground at the east of the wood were able to cut down many unfortunate enemy soldiers rapidly retreating from Bazentin le Grand village ahead of the 3rd Division attack on the right.

As the barrage was late lifting from the west face of the Snout, the forward rush of the assaulting troops had been delayed by some five minutes, which allowed the Germans in the main trench behind it the time to man their parapets. Although the centre of the advancing wave entered the German front line trench without difficulty, the left of the left company, which had been delayed, lost men to frontal rifle fire. Many men were killed and wounded before the German marksmen were eliminated by both flanking and frontal bombing.

A bomber, the Lewis gun team, and rifle fire, accounted for the occupants of a long 'tunnel' dug out in the second line trench, the bomber throwing in grenades at one end, the gunfire picking off the unfortunate doomed occupants scrambling out in panic from the other.

The enemy support trench, which ran down the slope across the wood about 100 yards inside the front edge before swinging into the arc known as Circus Trench, had almost been obliterated by the barrage. The company awaited the barrage to lift from the 'one hour line' before advancing to the north edge of the wood and digging in, signalling by the

Flatiron Copse cemetery. 13/King's Liverpools and 8/Devons lie side by side as they did in attack.

use of green flares at 4.35 am that their objective was secured. The 8/Devons' Battalion diary states, somewhat ambiguously and tersely, 'Very few prisoners taken'.

The support company started to advance at 3.45 am from their position near Flatiron Copse and took up position in the Snout Trench and its communication trenches, where some casualties were suffered as result of hostile shellfire. The company moved up later behind the creeping barrage to Circus Trench and onwards in a north easterly direction to occupy the bank facing north west overlooking Bazentin le Petit village, where they dug in. Patrols were sent out to clear any enemy pockets remaining in the north west segment of the wood.

The Battalion disposition after the advance was: three companies dug in from S.14.b.5.6 to S.14.b.8.8; and one company in support dug in 100 yards behind, plus an additional small party with 20/MGC at the strong post at S.15.a.4.7. An 8 inch howitzer, with ammunition, had been captured together with some trench mortars, and many rifles and equipment.

8/Devons casualties totalled: officers, three killed and five wounded; other ranks – 19 killed, 123 wounded, and 21 missing.

Attacking the front immediately left of the 8/Devons, and in the

8/Devons Lewis gunners resting after the attack. The Lewis gun carts were unpopular modes of transportation - unwieldly and difficult to move. Note the field guns and limbers moving behind.

first moments of the assault, troops on the right flank of B Company of the 2/Borders, just to the west side of Marlborough Trench, became bunched with some of the first line of 8/Devons, whose forward progress had been blocked by a wide, isolated tangle of thick wire. The close group became the target of concentrated frontal rifle fire and many died or were wounded at this point.

Having claimed the battered first line and the support trench through the wood without further effective opposition, and awaited there for the barrage to lift off the 'one hour line', the lead companies moved on to arrive at their sector of the north edge of Bazentin le Grand Wood at 4.42 am and signalled their presence with green flares. The line specified in orders for consolidation was under a thick tangle of splintered branches and wreckage so, to avoid delay, a bank about thirty yards ahead of the edge of the wood was selected instead, and quickly consolidated.

The troops remaining were not sufficient in number to man the defences satisfactorily and the troops of the following A Company were absorbed into the consolidated line. Several prisoners were captured from both lines, including a Colonel of the Lehr Regiment, and useable armaments included a machine gun, an automatic rifle, and a Lewis gun No. 20/BA2 which had been taken from a British aeroplane which had crashed near Bazentin le Grand Wood.

In the opening one hour and twenty minutes the battalion recorded casualties totalling two hundred and twenty one: two officers killed and one wounded; 23 other ranks killed, 124 wounded and 71 missing.

Troops of 22 Brigade then passed through the line to press the advance into Bazentin le Petit village.

At 4.30 am 2/Warwicks had moved forwards from their reserve position in the eastern corner of Mametz Wood, crossed the newly won German front line trench and reformed in their assembly position south of Bazentin le Grand Wood. They moved up through the defensive line established by 20 Brigade, and under heavy fire C Company, followed quickly by D Company, lead the assault to occupy Circus Trench and its communication trench, off which the barrage had just lifted. Consolidation of the positions started immediately, and the left flank line was extended along the track running beside Bazentin le Petit Wood.

2/RIR, following immediately behind, passed through 2/Warwicks positions and advanced against Bazentin le Petit village. A Company under Lieutenant Hegarty attacked towards the cemetery; C Company under Captain Tighe attacked through the village; B Company formed a left flank guard for the village attackers, with a defensive flank along the eastern edge of the wood to extend the defensive flank of

2/R.Warwicks; and D Company was held in reserve.

According to the Battalion War Diary of 2/RIR, Captain Tighe and his C Company started to attack the village before the barrage had completely lifted, trapping many of the enemy soldiers in bunkers and shelters, which were cleared by bombing parties. The commander and HQ staff of 16/Bavarian Regiment and over 200 men were captured, although whether or not this claim is in addition to those already captured by the Leicestershire Brigade during their earlier assault eastwards from the wood, is not clear. Certainly the 2/RIR suffered extremely heavy losses during their action, which were probably sustained pushing through the wrecked and dangerous ruins towards the eastern side of the village.

The factors governing this part of the attack on the village of Bazentin le Petit differed from those in the adjoining 21st Division sector, attacking the wood immediately west. The terrain demanding a much earlier effective use of machine guns. Strong points were established and emplacements constructed and the guns moved up

Position of 2/RIR at 8.15am. 22nd Infantry Brigade diary.

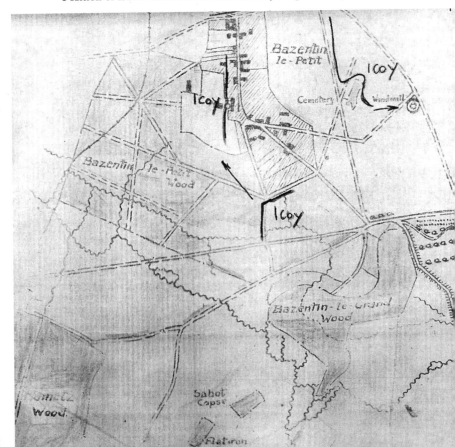

early to operate very effectively from forward covering positions as soon as 20 Brigade's objectives were secured.

At 5 am two guns of No.1 Section of 20/MGC under Lieutenant Lawley arrived at their objective at the road intersection north of Bazentin le Grand Wood, and the diary records that at 7.15 am at a range of 400 yards, 'about 40 killed', running from Bazentin le Petit village. Covered emplacements were to be constructed later at this position by 95/Field Company RE.

Nos. 1 and 3 Sections of 22/MGC moved forward at 5.15 am to support 2/RIR, No 1 Section in Circus Trench and No.3 Section first to the east side of Bazentin le Grand Wood and then on to a position outside the north east of the wood.

No 3 Section of 20/MGC, under Lieutenant Drew, at 6 am moved two guns forward via the eastern edge of Caterpillar Wood to the German second line trench, where they waited whilst the wood was scouted and confirmed as clear, before assuming, at 6.45 am, their appointed position on the west side of Bazentin le Grand Wood, about 100 yards south of the road.

The other two guns of the section moved to a position near Marlborough Wood to await deployment. Also at 6 am, two guns of No 4 Section under Lieutenant Whiteway moved via the eastern edge of Caterpillar Wood and Marlborough Trench to a position slightly in advance of that planned, on the consolidated bank in front of the south west tip of Bazentin le Grand Wood, in the line established by 2/Borders.

The ground captured in the first advance was thus rapidly guarded against anticipated counter-attacks, and cover provided, first for the push forward to secure the brigade objectives and then on towards High Wood.

At 7.40 am XIII Corps ordered the 2nd Indian Cavalry Division, forward from its position near Morlancourt, four miles south of Albert, and at 8.20 am the division moved off destined for action against the German High Wood positions. Over the slippery and uneven ground, pitted with shell holes, cut by old trenches and littered with the detritus of battle, progress was very slow indeed. The leading Brigade, The Secunderabad Cavalry (Brigadier-General C.L.Gregory) with one squadron of the Canadian Cavalry attached, and one field troop of Royal Engineers plus two armoured cars, did not arrive south of Montauban until past midday.

At 8.50 am Lieutenant-General Horne, commander of XV Corps, issued his follow up orders:

The 7th Division would relieve the 2nd Indian Cavalry Division in

High Wood. The 21st Division would move northwards and clear enemy communication trenches between Bazentin le Petit and the light railway tracks to Martinpuich. This would be linked to an advance agreed with the GOC III Corps (Lieutenant-General Pulteney) on the German second line positions west of Bazentin le Petit Wood, to be undertaken jointly by the 21st Division (XV Corps) and the 1st Division (III Corps). In co-ordination with this joint advance the 34th Division would attack towards Poziéres. 7th Division Field Artillery was brought up to Caterpiller Valley during the morning, and 1/3 Durham Field Company RE, with the pioneers, worked hard to improve the tracks in the rear areas, to facilitate the easier and speedier carriage of ammunition and supplies to the front. During the morning 54/Field Company RE moved into Bazentin le Petit, and 95/Field Company RE to Bazentin le Grand Wood, both with companies from 14/Northumberland (Pioneers) attached, to construct strong-points urgently, to consolidate positions, cut access routes, and to repair tramway and roads, as well as detonating unexploded bombs.

Lieutenant-General Horne's further battle plan, for various reasons, did not materialise.

By 7.30 am after severe fighting at close quarters, 2/RIR, assisted in some part by D Company 2/Warwicks, were in control of Bazentin le Petit village, although still under fire and suffering casualties from machine guns from east of the village and, in the northern end of the village were caught in artillery fire from both German and British batteries.

At 8.15 am the cemetery was wrested from the enemy by A Company 2/RIR lead by Lieutenant Hegarty, and a patrol with Lewis gunners was sent to attack and to occupy the windmill. A defensive line from the cemetery to the crossroads at the north of Bazentin le Petit village (S.8.a.8.7) was formed, and a strong point established at the windmill.

About the same time, the left flank of the village came under fire from the direction of the wood, and D Company 2/RIR moved into and through the wood in extended order. After eventually meeting up with troops of the Leicestershire Brigade, they returned to battalion reserve.

The troops on the left flank extended the line into the clearing between the wood and village, and although some connection was established with troops in the north of the wood, the situation was very confused, with severe shelling on this northern area repeatedly forcing the Leicesters out of position.

Moving forward unusually early, 95/Field Coy RE completed their

A strong point was established at the windmill. The site (above) as viewed from Bazentin le Petit communal cemetery, and the windmill (left) before destruction. The windmill was the scene of terrible close quarter fighting on 14 July.

move section by section, at five minute intervals, to rendezvous at Caterpillar Wood by 6.30 am. At 6.45 am they received orders by runner from 22 Brigade HQ to proceed immediately to complete their allotted tasks, building strong points at the west end of Bazentin le Grand Wood, another just outside the wood, two machine gun emplacements at the cross roads S.14.b.9.9, and a strong point north of the road. All sections with their supporting pioneers, were clear of the wood by 7.30 am, but the move accounted for Captain Jones, killed, and several infantry pioneers wounded.

The CO and four men of No 2 Company 7th Division Signals tried in vain to establish communication with Divisional HQ at Pommiers Redoubt from Bazentin le Grand Wood by use of signal lamp. The attempt failed due to bad visibility, a recurrent swirling yellow fog blocking signals, and about 7.30 am the attempt was abandoned. The Snout escarpment was subjected to a bombardment by a 5.9' battery and the exposed position was becoming progressively more precarious. The lamp was left with the Battalion HQ of 2/Warwicks in Mametz Wood, to enable contact back to White Trench at such time as became possible, their telephonic contact with 22 Brigade HQ being unreliable and subject to prolonged interruptions.

The commanding officer of 2/RIR reported repeatedly from 9.45 am onwards, that enemy machine gun fire from the wood was causing danger to his left flank, and that he feared a counter-attack. Although rogue guns were still operating from the wood, this prolonged fire was more likely to have been from the strong point just north of the wood, which was causing, and would continue to cause, many problems.

On the east flank at about this time Captain Wasey and B Company of 2/Warwicks patrolling east along the road towards Bazentin le Grand, suffered casualties from machine gun fire. They fell into, and then moved eastwards along, the gully which runs from the north end of Bazentin le Grand Wood just south of the road, and discovered a group of dead 1/Northumberland Fusiliers and German soldiers at the cross roads. They saw an approaching group of about 30 German infantrymen advancing across the elevated ground from the direction of High Wood and realised that the area of orchards and ditches to the north east of Bazentin le Grand bristled with enemy troops. Whilst the company engaged the attention of the enemy from the road, Sergeant Pulteney, as scout, scrambled towards the village of Bazentin le Grand to alert 3rd Division troops as to the situation. 1/Northumberland Fusiliers (9 Brigade) were in fact well aware of the position and, upon the arrival of bombers and 9/Stokes Gun Battery, quickly moved to combine in a successful attack, forcing the occupying German troops

The engagement against the last defenders by 1/Northumberland Fusiliers and Captain Wasey's 2/Warwicks.

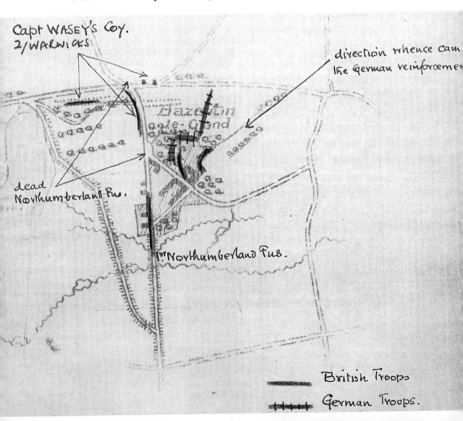

to withdraw towards High Wood. During the return journey to his company, accompanied by a Northumberland Fusilier, Sergeant Pulteney located a machine gun post in a cellar. Forcing entry, they killed the lone machine gunner, and captured four machine guns.

The commanding officer 2/RIR was urgently requested by message at 10.20 am to send reinforcements to their left flank. In response, the reserve D Company, plus a platoon from B Company which was guarding the east flank, were ordered to assist. The continuing bombardment of the village and wood, with additional rifle fire from the wood, was rapidly reducing the defensive capability of the defenders, and additional support was requested from brigade.

Heavy bombardments on the woods for an hour by the Germans starting about 10 am was followed by counter attacks. At 11.00 am a message warned of further enemy troop movement from High Wood and the imminent possibility of counter attack. In response to an urgent request from Brigade HQ for assistance in the area of the cemetery, one of the guns of No 1 Section of 20/MGC from the south west tip of the wood moved to the road embankment at the cross roads north of Bazentin le Grand Wood (S.15.a.10.98), and with additional fire from the No 3 Section guns at the north east of Bazentin le Grand Wood, arrested enemy progress from the right, assisted by information from an artillery forward observation officer.

At about 11.30 am a large counter-action started, the main body aimed against the northern boundary of Bazentin le Petit Wood and village, with columns of Germans attacking in line from the direction of Martinpuich and High Wood. As a result of what must have been extremely fierce and bloody close combat, many dead of both sides were subsequently discovered in the areas.

This counter-strike, with great numbers concentrated against the north edge of the wood between the tramway and the village, pushed back the defence line, the north east segment of the wood rapidly filled with attackers, who then pushed eastwards towards the village, under sporadic flank fire from a tenuous defensive line relocated across the north part of the clearing The infantrymen pushed back from their positions in the north east of Bazentin le Petit Wood, and gathering on the eastern edge, were blocking the line of fire of the No 1 Section machine gun remaining at the south west tip of Bazentin le Grand Wood. As a result this gun was quickly moved back to the crest of the rise (at S.14.d.30.80), in order to fire over the heads of the British infantry grouped at the edge of Bazentin le Petit Wood and to hinder enemy progress.

At 11.45 am 2/RIR moved two platoons from B Company and two platoons from D Company west from the village towards the north east of the wood, in answer to the urgent call for support, and immediately met the opposing attackers pressing eastwards. A short, very intense encounter ensued, killing Lieutenant Finlay and leaving many more dead and wounded, before the remainder of 2/RIR could withdraw back into the village.

The counter-attacking forces fought into the village, pushing back 2/RIR eastwards and outflanking C Company, positioned along the northern extremity. In the fighting which followed Captain Tighe was killed by machine gun fire from the direction of the wood, and Lieutenant Stuttaford and CSM Smith were seriously wounded.

With the German counter-attackers again in control of the north end of the village, A and D Companies of 24/Manchesters (Pioneers), who had been working on the construction of a keep in the centre of the village, were hurriedly pressed back into their primary role as infantrymen.

Seconded by the commanding officer 2/RIR to assist in repelling invaders, Second Lieutenant W Soward (11/East Surreys attached 24/Manchesters) with a platoon, moved westwards to fight into the north east of Bazentin le Petit Wood, and in due course reported the wood clear, but that the enemy still occupied the trench at S.8.a.8.3 (this is now the line of the path to the military cemetery). Meanwhile Lieutenant Bateman, with another platoon, moved east to help, by sustained rifle fire, to force encroaching attackers back from the cemetery.

Remaining at the keep, Captain CH Lee and the rest of A and D Companies, 24/Manchesters whilst all becoming involved in the defence, continued construction as well as possible under machine gun and shell attack. As a result of these engagements completion of the work almost needless to say, was recorded as delayed. During the engagement Lieutenant Andrew and five other ranks were killed, and Second Lieutenant Soward and 44 other ranks wounded.

The Germans who had reoccupied the northern part of the village were eventually driven out during the early afternoon. A Company of 2/Warwicks, lead by Lieutenant Fowler and Lieutenant Cory-Wright, scrapping northwards, moved block by block, forcing back the encroaching German raiding parties. After very severe hand to hand fighting, during which many losses were incurred, with the assistance of 100 men of the 20/Manchesters who were in the village at the time as a carrying party for 54/Field Company RE, and with the remainder of A Company plus two platoons from D Company of 2/RIR counter-attacking from the east, the ruins of the village were once more reclaimed. At the northern extremity an overturned cart used as a barricade enabled a group of withdrawing Germans to hold out and to cause many casualties before they attempted to escape, only to be cut down and killed by machine gun fire from the direction of the cemetery.

Starting very shortly after the assault in the north, the north east flank was also assailed by the counter-attacking forces, concentrated towards the cemetery and extending from the windmill down to the Bazentin le Grand cross roads. 2/RIR was extended on all fronts and 2/Warwicks were fighting to hold the east flank. A defensive artillery barrage was called for on the High Wood side of the cemetery, but the Windmill, defended by Lieutenant Deane and men of A Company 2/RIR, was overrun and occupied by the German attackers, at the same time as the enemy had penetrated and were fighting back through the north of the village.

Sometime about 12.30 pm, a disorganised group of between 300 and 400 dishevelled men from mixed regiments were reported hurriedly leaving Bazentin le Petit village, driven out by shell fire and the German attackers. The War Diary of 95/Field Company RE and other records state that the RSM 2/RIR and the commanding officer and CSM 95/Coy RE attempted in vain to stop the exodus. The War Diary of 2/RIR states that the retreat was stopped by Captain Lowe, their Adjutant.

A party of about thirty Germans attacked down the sunken road between the windmill and the cemetery, threatening the south east defences of the village but, according to the Battalion War Diary, were stopped by a party of 2/RIR, moving out from their battalion HQ and lead by their Adjutant, Captain Lowe. All the invading Germans

Dead Germans lie in a sunken road.

perished in cross fire from 2/RIR holding the cemetery and the machine gun post at the north of Bazentin le Grand Wood.

Captain Wasey, 2/Warwicks who had first observed the oncoming waves of German counter-attackers some time after the combined action with 1/Northumberland Fusiliers at the crossroads, had positioned his B Company of 2/Warwicks in a defensive flank along the sunken road running from the cross roads towards the windmill, up to about 100 yards south of it, and was there joined by parts of A and D Companies. Intense rifle fire, together with fire from a Lewis gun mounted on top of an overturned howitzer to the north of Bazentin le Grand Wood, and other machine gun fire, halted the German advance here at about 200 yards range.

At 12.35 pm the sappers of 95/Field Company RE, with pioneers constructing the strong point at the intersection north of Bazentin le Grand Wood (at S.15.a.3.9), and those building the machine gun emplacement nearby, had to interrupt their labours to take up arms to assist fighting off the counter-attack from the direction of the windmill. Their tasks were eventually completed at 7.30 pm, when the exhausted engineers and pioneers returned to bivouac at Caterpiller Wood.

The body of the officer commanding the defence of the windmill was later found stripped and mutilated, together with three of his men who had been shot dead at very close range. The hate and determined ferocity on both sides was extreme and without quarter during these relentless exchanges.

German counter-attacks against Bazentin-Le-Petit 14 July, 1916.

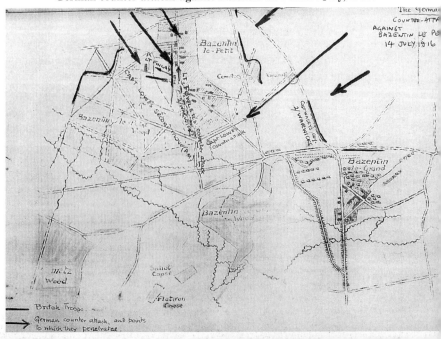

2/RIR came under increasing pressure on the eastern flank from additional German forces attacking from the direction of High Wood towards the cemetery, and just before 1 pm 1/RWF, under the command of Captain EH Dadd, were ordered forwards from their reserve position to attack the flank of the German counter-attack from the south. They moved up over the high ground on the eastern side of Bazentin le Grand Wood under constant shell fire, A and C Companies in the lead, with B and D in support, and with the bombing company and four Lewis guns in reserve. The brigade had additionally placed four Maxim guns of 22/MGC and a battery of artillery at the disposal of the battalion, such was the seriousness of the threat as viewed by Divisional HQ.

At 2.35 pm Second Lieutenant J Dadd, A Company, 1/RWF, reported that 2/RIR had been forced back by the counter-attack from the high ground between the cemetery and the windmill. Four machine guns from the post on the east of Bazentin le Grand Wood at S.15.a.6.8 manned by No. 4 section of 22/Machine Gun Company swept the area between the windmill and High Wood, whilst the lead companies of the 1/RWF reoccupied and consolidated the cemetery – windmill line, linking with 2/RIR at the cemetery. On pressing forward northwards, C Company on the right immediately came under sustained machine gun fire from the elevated ground ahead.1/RWF manned and stood fast on the line cemetery – windmill, and also reinforced the troops in the sunken road to the road junction at the north of Bazentin le Grand, where two extra machine guns had been relocated.

Before 3.30 pm action on the eastern flank had completely ceased, the counter attack had been stopped and held by the reorganised defence line, well serviced by the automatic weapon placements, and the remaining German attackers had withdrawn, leaving many dead and seriously wounded scattered across the ground rising towards High Wood.

1/RWF casualties included Second Lieutenant GP Morgan and Lieutenant RHB Baynes killed and buried near the windmill, Captain EJ Greaves, Captain GL Compton-Smith, Lieutenant CN Smith, and Second Lieutenant SLL Brunicardi wounded, and 7 other ranks killed, 28 wounded and 6 missing..

At about 2 pm Captain Lowe had organised a contingent of his 2/RIR in a sweep through the south east of Bazentin le Petit Wood to remove any remaining infiltrators. Moving from the eastern section of

Crucifix corner to the Windmill. The line of 1/RWF on 14 July 1916.

BAZENTIN LE PETIT WOOD   BAZENTIN LE PETIT VILLAGE   THE CEMETERY AND QUARRY   THE WINDMILL

LINE HELD BY 1/RWF

the Forest Trench line, between Hedge Alley and the road, northwards in extended line towards and across the clearing, they reported that a defence line had been established manned by men from various regiments along the northern face of the clearing, through which the contingent passed, and moved on to the northern face of the wood.

A partially dug and undefended trench from the north east of the wood was strewn with countless bodies of men of the Leicestershire Brigade and was, according to their Battalion War Diary, then manned by 2/RIR until the arrival of 2/Gordons at around 6.45 pm. This claim would seem to be seriously contradicted by the interchange of messages which took place after the arrival later of 2/Gordons and which are quoted verbatim later in this chapter, although such was the frenzied and chaotic activity in this area, that the occupying 2/RIR could well have been overwhelmed in turn by a German assault back to the west from the north of the village.

My father spoke of a Leicesters' trench being destroyed by shellfire, and that the exhausted troops whom he had ordered to entrench on a new line a short distance away, much to their disgust and with much swearing and cursing, were eternally grateful when the old line erupted under an extremely intense bombardment, and was subsequently overrun by 'a horde of bloody Jerries'.

Starting at 2.30 pm 1/East Yorks, moving up from reserve, followed in the tracks of 2/RIR without encountering opposition, to take up positions reinforcing 7/Leicesters in the north of Bazentin le Petit Wood.

At about 2 pm 20 Brigade received orders from the 7th Division HQ to move reserves forward to sort out the confused situation in Bazentin le Petit village and the north east of the wood.

An entry in 22 Brigade diary timed at 12.20 pm, however, advises that the 2/Gordon's had been ordered to clear up the situation in Bazentin le Petit Wood, though this may be a misplaced request from them to Division.

According to the 7th Division Signals Company report, when 2/Gordon Highlanders were called forward urgently to ensure the German counter-attack was unsuccessful, the Signal Company ran a line to the advanced HQ position of 2/Borders and, as the precise relocation of the 2/Gordons HQ was not known, a message sent by runner requested two men be sent to 2/Borders HQ to pick up the line. The men detailed failed to arrive. A second attempt at connection was made as soon as the whereabouts of the new HQ was advised, and a cable was run out to the south west corner of Bazentin le Petit Wood. Unfortunately this was severely damaged by a squadron of the cavalry brigade galloping through between the woods to charge towards High Wood; the cable was severed in several places, but at least visual communication was by then established. The line was eventually relaid, and telephone connection was opened just before 8.30 pm!

22 Brigade War Diary records: At 5.45p.m it was reported that the 2/RIR were holding all of the village, but had lost heavily.

Having waited in reserve in the Hammerhead part of Mametz Wood since the previous afternoon, and endured the discomfort of sustained bombardment throughout the morning, at 3.20 pm on 14 July, the commanding officer 2/Gordon Highlanders, Lieutenant Colonel Gordon, received the following message from Brigadier-General CJ Deverell commanding 20 Brigade.

> The ROYAL IRISH of the 22nd Infantry Brigade in BAZENTIN-LE-PETIT have been counter-attacked from the Northern end of BAZENTIN-LE-PETIT WOOD and the enemy has gained a footing in some of the houses. You will move at once to BAZENTIN LE PETIT passing through all troops on the road and will attack the N.E. part of the WOOD moving N.W. from the open space immediately W of the words B.M. 147. The 21st Division has been warned of your movement and will attack the N.W. part of the WOOD moving due N. You will employ only such strength as you consider essential but will move up the whole of your battalion so as to be ready to use it all or as much of it as may be required. The situation is critical and urgent. A sketch is attached shewing area to be cleared and occupied by you.

Bazentin-Le-Petit village 1916.

The battalion quickly formed up and advanced, under continuing shell bursts, in two lines of companies in column of platoons, led by D Company on the left, A Company on the right, B Company on the left of the support line, with C Company on the right. By 4 pm the battalion reached the fortified bank some 30 yards north of Bazentin le Grand Wood and sent out scouts to ascertain the situation. The report back at about 5 pm was that the Leicesters were holding the north edge of Bazentin le Petit Wood, (with right flank at S.8.a.8.7), and that *the village was clear of enemy*. D Company was ordered to advance to establish a line from S.8.a.5.3 to S.8.a.8.7 (across the north edge of the village to link with the Leicesters on the left).

In fact the enemy were still in occupation of the northern part of the village. Three platoons of D Company, with the fourth in support, attacked and overwhelmed the enemy, cleared the village, and sent 22 prisoners back to the compound. The remnants of the severely mauled 2/RIR were mustered at the keep. An interesting exchange of messages followed between the officer commanding 2/Gordons and Brigade HQ, as recorded in the summary report of 2/Gordon Highlanders, and appendix to the diary of 20 Brigade.

1st Message: *6.30 p.m. O.C. 2nd Gordons*

LEICESTER Bde about 200 strong holding top LE PETIT etc WOOD, I have no map so cannot give exact position. We are not in touch with our right yet but have scouts watching the right front and a right flank guard about one platoon strong. We are weakest on the right as we are not in touch with VII Division.

Sgd: S.R.Ellwood,Lt.

2nd Message: *6.55 p.m.*

Am in position N.and E sides of BAZENTIN LE PETIT S.8.a.8.7. to S.8.b.2.6. and in touch with LEICESTERSHIRE REGT on my left but no one is on my right. Send another company to occupy remainder of E side of BAZENTIN LE PETIT.

Sgd O.C. 'D' Company.

3rd Message: *7.30 p.m.*

A party of mixed regiments with 4 machine guns are holding N side of CEMETERY. There is another small party at the WINDMILL S.9.c.4.9... None between my right and CEMETERY.

Sgd O.C. 'D' Company.

4th Message: *3.30.a.m. (15 July)*

Have extended my line from crossroads to N.W. corner of village S.8.a.6.7. the line is continue as from S.7.b.7.4. along edge of WOOD to S.8.a.6.3. then Northwards W side of village to S.8.a.6.7. then E to S.8.b.4.8. from there a straight line to N.W. corner of cemetery S.8.b.8.2. Regiments left to right 8th and 9th LEICESTERS YORKSHIRES LEICESTERS GORDONS MANCHESTERS. All quiet.

Sgd O.C. 'D' Company.

A special note has been added at the end of the 2/Gordons report stating,

> *Considerable delay was caused on the battalion arriving at S.14.b.2.5. owing to the fact that no information on the general situation could be obtained until the battalion scouts had gained touch with the LEICESTERSHIRE BRIGADE. A party of the ROYAL IRISH were thought to be holding the N.E. corner of the village B.M.150.7, but on D company advancing this was found to be incorrect and necessitated an extension of their front.*

At 7.05 pm the gap reported in the line between Bazentin le Petit and the cemetery was filled by one and a half companies of 20/Manchesters, who were severely bombarded during the night.

About 8 am on 14 July 20/Manchesters, in 22 Brigade reserve, had moved forward from Fritz Trench to occupy White Trench, where they were heavily shelled with both HE and gas shells, and needed to wear goggles continuously throughout the day. C and D Companies were ordered up to support 2/Warwicks and 2/RIR in Bazentin le Petit village, and arriving at about 7 pm, were directed to hold the line from the north of the village to the cross roads directly east, suffering severe casualties from shellfire. During the morning of the 15th they were relieved by 2/Warwicks, and returned to rendezvous with the rest of their battalion on the south edge of Bazentin le Petit Wood.

2/Gordons were relieved during the morning of 15 July by the

Argyll and Sutherland Highlanders, and arrived back at the HALT after midnight to bivouac. They recorded their casualties for the day as, four officers wounded, 14 other ranks killed, 45 wounded, and five missing. Lieutenant Colonel Gordon was killed in action on 20 July during the attack on High Wood from Bazentin le Petit.

The commander of 20 Brigade, Brigadier General Deverell, wrote in his battle report

> *In accordance with orders received from Divisional HQ, I directed the O.C.2/Gordon Highlanders to move his battalion up to assist in the capture of North East portions of the Wood, and explained the situation to him in writing and sent a sketch of the area allotted to him to clear. The situation as received from Divisional H.Q., was found to be not exactly as stated, and, it was found that the northern end of BAZENTIN LE PETIT VILLAGE was not held at all by our troops, and that it was necessary to clear not only the N. E. portion of BAZENTIN LE PETIT WOOD but also the northern half of BAZENTIN LE PETIT VILLAGE. These areas were cleared by 2/Gordon Highlanders and 22 prisoners taken, but when this had been accomplished at 6.30 p.m. 2/Gordon Highlanders, although in touch with the Brigade of the 21st Division on our left in the WOOD, were not in touch with any troops of the 7th Division on our right - a gap existing as far as up to the CEMETERY.*

At 8.15 pm orders were issued by 22 Brigade that 2/Warwicks were to hold the line from the north of Bazentin le Petit village to the cemetery, and 1/RWF from there to the north end of Bazentin le Grand Village. Nos.1 and 3 Sections of 22/MGC were withdrawn to Mametz Wood, No 2 Section was in the line north east of Bazentin le Petit and No 4 Section with 1/RWF in the vicinity of the windmill.

22 Brigade casualties for 14 July 1916 are recorded as follows:

	Officers		**Other ranks**			
(Killed/Wounded/Missing)	K	W	K	W	M	Total
2/Warwicks	1	5	21	125	75	227
2/RIR	3	9	24	208	86	332
1/RWF	1	4	16	125	15	161
20/Manchesters	Nil	2	14	142	52	210
22/MGC	Nil	2	3	21	4	30
TM Battery	Nil	Nil	Nil	2	Nil	2

Chapter Seven

THE ATTACK OF THE 21st DIVISION: 14 JULY 1916

At 3.20 am on 14 July the final countdown to zero hour started with the intensive artillery bombardment, prior to which the leading assault troops had crawled forward as close as they dared to the German front line (Flatiron Trench), some in this sector as close as fifty yards. Giles Eyre gives a dramatic description of the launch of the attack:

A terrific thrumming din brought us to our feet with a jerk and we ran to the parapets. In the murk of late night the flashing red glares of the bursts were enveloping the whole length of the German advanced and support lines, throwing the scene into awesome and vivid relief. The German front system appeared as a blazing, blinding wall of terrible dancing and leaping ruddy flames. Tongues of fire licked up, rising into the air, and the wood became etched in crimson light. Huge spouts of earth, as if pushed by giant hands spouted high into the air continually, the undulating clouds lit momentarily by the yellow and crimson stabs of the bursts. Green and red rockets soared up far over the trees from the tortured heaving enemy trenches. All previous bombardments appeared to me like childs-play in comparison. I glanced around at the awe-struck pale-faced men peering over the parapets with stark amazement and fear in their glaring

eyes...The roar of the whizzing shells overhead and the awful noise of the crashes made all speech impossible...Minute after minute the noise increased until our ear drums hammered like mad, and the quivering air, laden with the acrid tang of explosives, became difficult to breathe. My heart was thumping heavily, rapidly. My pulses beat quicker and even our trenches shook and quivered and rocked about at the shock of this tremendous burst of fire...Most of the men were gripped by unplumbed horror, and yet at the same time uplifted to the extent that space and time ceased to have any meaning. We were living in a world where flames, pandemonium and death held undisputed sway and our living bodies were as nothing...The guns with a last soul blasting sound increased their rate of fire and hurled a final, awful thundering blast of shell at the heaps of heaving earth in front of us and then, as if hurled into oblivion by some unknown force, suddenly ceased.

The instant of profound silence was more impressive than all the noise our ears had been subjected to...then the shrill blasting of whistles as the lines of the attacking infantry swarmed towards the wrecked German line. At the same time, with another terrific surge of sound, the guns, having lengthened their ranges, hurled their massed loads of death into and beyond the wood, with rending crashes.[10]

When at 3.25 am the barrage lifted forwards, the leading troops swarmed over towards the German fortifications. The enemy wire on this front had been well cut by the artillery and caused no problems, but many casualties were inflicted by strategically placed machine guns, some situated in tall trees in the wood ahead.

6/Leicesters on the right front with 7/Leicesters to their left, each with one company of 8/Leicesters in support, led the attack on Bazentin le Petit Wood, entering the enemy front trenches soon after the first lift of the barrage. Private Jack Horner recalled his brief experience of the battle:

As we lay and waited for the signal to Go! I had a look round. In the far distance, on the right, we could see our objective, the village of Bazentin, or what was left of it, and a large farmhouse. Our platoon officer Lieutenant Smith, raised his arm, pointed forward, and shouted 'Go!' There was no shelling, but a machine gun and four men, appeared from nowhere, in front of the farmhouse, and held up the entire centre, but we on the right flank were able to push forward. From upper windows of the

farmhouse, the Germans were shooting us down, as if we were
rabbits in a field.

The rifle fire from the farmhouse was intense, and I got a
bullet through my right fore-arm. If you are hit by a high velocity
bullet, it's rather like a red hot poker going through your flesh,
and the force with which it travelled knocked me back, and flung
my rifle yards away. There was not a great deal of blood, but my
right hand went dead and immovable. The Field Dressing Station
in Mametz Wood was very busy – the Doctors, orderlies, and
stretcher bearers working flat out, in what appeared to be
organised chaos, amid the many mutilated men who needed
attention. After waiting some time my arm was bandaged, I was
given an injection, and labelled 'Walking Wounded'.[2]

He was to survive all of this fighting and a very serious wound at
Passchendaele. His memories of the war were still very vivid when
interviewed by Nigel Cave, in 1983.

The building described as the farmhouse was almost certainly the
ruined Lamarck House which stood in the clearing on what is now the
site of the Lamarck memorial.

The first two lines of assault, A wave, of 6/Leicesters, following
closely behind the barrage, stormed and entered the heavily battered
front line trench almost as soon as the barrage lifted, and captured
about 30 prisoners. Considerable casualties however, were caused by
machine gun fire both from an emplacement at the south east corner of
Bazentin le Petit Wood, and particularly by deadly flank fire from
Bazentin le Grand Wood, the 7th Division not having yet been able to
access and clear the northern part of that wood, which lay behind their
artillery 'one hour' lift line. Giles Eyre provides a detailed description

After hastily stumbling across No Man's Land undisturbed for
the first fifty yards, men began to drop as machine guns began
their destructive raking...Once more with a high shrill cheer the
straggling wave of men hurled itself forward, to be met by a blast
of fire. Unfortunates were pitching forward at every step, and
flopping down like empty sacks, writhing, twisting, and moaning.
The ground here was a mass of holes and dead men, sand-bags,
and scattered, blasted bushes and wood...hurling another flight
of grenades, we slithered down within a few yards of the trench,
with a machine-gun spluttering and roaring close in front.

Trr-trr-trr spoke the Lewis behind us as, with a last rush we
flung ourselves over the obstacle. Blam! snapped a pistol shot
close to me, and then I found myself standing over a writhing

German on the ground. I had pinned him with my bayonet! Crashes and shots, shouts and scurry all round me. The subaltern yelling like mad – a confused splatter of machine-guns, rifle shots, running men, cries, groans, the slam of shrapnel howling and whistling. Groups of men are lining the trench, and more are crowding in all the time. Wounded Huns and some of our boys are moaning and staggering in near us. Dead men, hideously mangled, are now being revealed to our eyes by the rising sun. The wood looms menacingly before us, just a clump of interlaced foliage and broken, scarred stumps, with the enemy lurking within it. The Hun gun is slap in front of us, somewhere in the bushes at the edge of the trees, another twenty yards onwards. 'Sling some grenades and rush it,' cries the officer as the Lewis gun ceases fire. We hurl grenades, and, as they burst, yell like devils out of hell and rush. We just catch sight of a couple of scuttling grey figures and reach the gun. It is lying over lop-sided, a Boche, covered in blood, twitching and swaying drunkenly over it. Another flat on his back in the complete abandon of death with knees drawn up and arms out-flung. A caved-in dugout entrance, hidden by leaves and fallen branches, and a pain-laden voice: 'Englishman, mercy!' A young German with white, scared face and holding one hand up feebly is half lying, half leaning by the dug-out, with Rodwell standing over him with his bayonet. [10]

Following on immediately, the second two lines of assault, B wave, hurrying through the sprays of machine gun bullets, pushed on over

A dead German lies next to his machine gun. Knocking out these guns were a priority for advancing troops.

The machine gun post in front of the wood caused many casualties to the first wave of attacking 7/Leicesters.

Flatiron Trench; by 4 am they claimed possession of the German second line trench, also greatly damaged, and sparsely manned.

The company to the right set up blocks in both trenches, and established a flank defence, and the third and fourth lines charged and bombed the machine gun post in the south east corner of Bazentin le Petit Wood, killing the gunners and commandeering the two guns

Adjacent to 6/Leicesters, A Company of 7/Leicesters, on the extreme right of their sector, had also entered the front trench from a short distance immediately after the intense artillery barrage lifted. D Company on the left, near the tramway, although not so close, was able to crawl up to the parapet and rush the trench, but not before being strafed and held up by machine gun fire from the west. Attacking the centre front, B and C Companies had not approached so close to the barrage and had allowed the enemy time to man both his parapet and an emplacement containing three machine guns near Right Alley. As a result, they were pinned down and severely mauled by concentrated fire for some twenty minutes, until bombers working inwards from the right flank destroyed the post and silenced the guns, one remaining undamaged.

The defenders in the first line (Flatiron Trench) tried to fight off the fierce attack, but those not caught in their bunkers, on realising the inevitability of being overwhelmed, fled into Forest Trench, from where many surrendered. Some ran on, chancing their luck in getting through the curtain of shellfire which had lifted into the wood beyond.

Urged forward by the subaltern, Giles Eyre and the 2/KRRC bombing party, minus the lance corporal and the bomb carriers, and with now but three Lewis gunners in close attendance, crashed on through the tangle towards Forest Trench

Sounds of battle all over the place. The dull thud, thud of grenades, the rat-tat-tat of machine-guns and the sharp crack of scattered rifle shots, come to us from all sides. The Leicesters are attacking the line of the wood to our left, but seem to be hung up, for all of a sudden a wave of rapid fire breaks out from them. We inch on, grenades in hands crawling on hands and knees. Crash!

German machine gun post, captured July 1916, surrounded by mixed German and British equipment.

A German stick grenade bursts just beyond us. [10]

At 3.50 am the second, B, wave of 7/Leicesters passed over the first trench, drawing after them the remaining troops of the first line of A wave to assist in the consolidation of the much damaged second trench (Forest Trench), which was secured with little resistance. The second line of A wave remained at the first trench, clearing bunkers and rooting out any troublesome Germans who remained concealed. CSM Geary, returning to inspect the clearing operations in Flatiron Trench, discovered a number of armed fugitives missed in the chaos.

The left of D Company, 7/Leicesters advanced too quickly beyond Forest Trench, and sustained losses under the creeping barrage, retired and bearing left re-established contact with 8/Leicesters, covering the left flank, near Aston Trench.

Of the 7/Leicesters officers, Captain Wright and Captain Gifford, Lieutenant Burdett, Lieutenant Hollis, Lieutenant Abbott, and Second Lieutenants Newton, Gutteridge, and Bam, had all been killed, along with many of their soldiers, in the fiery hell of the dark dawn before reaching their first objective. Second Lieutenant Evans was by now the only officer in B Company, Second Lieutenant Reed was the lone surviving officer of C Company, whilst in D Company no officers at all remained.

The 110 Brigade front viewed from the Snout. The German front line trench ran on a line almost straight down the centre of the picture from the front of Bazentin-Le-Petit Wood

Immediately following the barrage lift the first two platoons of D Company of 8/Leicesters, flanking the left of the assault, with extra bombers and raiders in the front ranks, hurriedly advanced across their attack front, to the left of the tramway, having crawled under the cover of the barrage to positions about 200 yards in front of the German front line. Their objectives were to capture Villa Trench for a distance of about 100 yards west from the tramway, and to form a block therein, then to repeat the operation in Aston Trench – the support trench about 200 yards further ahead, clearing on the way the communication trench between the two known as Left Alley. The line of advance was directly in the line of fire of German machine guns from emplacements situated at Contalmaison Villa and the strongpoint north west of the wood. The first two platoons and the follow up platoons of the storming 8/Leicesters were extensively cut up. Many were killed crossing the open ground, all company officers being casualties. On reaching Villa Trench the remaining troops encountered little opposition, bombing parties cleared dug outs and the remaining raiders fought along the communications trench and took Aston Trench. Fleeing occupants were shot by the Lewis Gun team, which had been rapidly brought into the action and, competently led by the company NCOs, the ground gained was quickly consolidated and the link with the 7/Leicesters on their right was re-established.

944 Sergeant Alfred Adams DCM. Leicesters was given this Gillette fety razor by a friend who had a emonition of death on the eve of the ttle. The case in Sgt Adam's breast cket was struck by a bullet and ved his life. His friend was killed.

110 Brigade War Diary notes.

4.00 am. Enemy first and second lines were in our occupation, and some progress

105

A photograph of Lt Col ACH Robinson, DSO, at the 20 Light Division memorial at Langemark (Belgium), near where he won his DSO in 1917. At Bazentin he was a sergeant in the 8/Leicesters, where he was wounded (amongst other things, the tip of his nose was shot away). He was puzzled by the cheering crowds when being evacuated through a large town in a bus – and remembered it was Bastille Day! The day after this photograph was taken, on 11 November 1984, he died.

in consolidating had been made, this was difficult owing to the trenches having been much damaged by our artillery. The enemy defensive wire was found to have been well cut throughout.

At 4.a.m. the Brigade was disposed as follows :- 6th Bn Leics Regt on right and 7th Bn Leics Regt on left in FOREST and FLATIRON trenches, D company 8th Bn Leics Regt in LEFT ALLEY with blocks in ASTON and VILLA trenches. – one company 8th Bn in support of D company in North of Mametz Wood, immediately west of tramway. Two companies 8th Bn supporting the 6th and 7th Bns were lying in open ground East of MAMETZ WOOD and in Northern edge of MAMETZ WOOD respectively. 9th Bn Leics Regt and 1st Bn East Yorks in reserve at SE end of MAMETZ WOOD. 110 M.G.Coy – 2 sections in WOOD TRENCH – 2 sections in QUADRANGLE SUPPORT Trench. 110 T.M.Bty – 4 guns in N.E.Corner MAMETZ WOOD – 2 guns in S.E.end of MAMETZ WOOD – 2 guns near FRICOURT.

Within twenty minutes of arrival, leaving three platoons in Forest Trench, and still suffering the flank fire from the emplacement in Bazentin le Grand Wood, the rest of 6/Leicesters on the right pushed forward in a fifteen minutes struggle towards the 'one hour line', cautiously following as closely as they dare. Giles Eyre graphically describes the chaos of battle:

The Lewis gun opens fire quickly, and we make another rush, only to crash against a barrier of barbed wire stretched and tangled between the trees. Somehow we get over the wire, our clothes tearing and the barbs scratching at our bodies and equipment, and we run slap-bang into another gun just behind. Germans jump up and come at us. For a moment there is a flurry of figures, half seen, hazy faces loom in front of me. I push forward my rifle and let go, working the bolt automatically, and then, as I empty my magazine, slash forward with my bayonet...I hear the short, sharp bark of the subaltern's pistol, and suddenly trip over the gun *and fall headlong over a struggling and kicking German, who tries to make a grab at me.*

Short sharp bursts of fire, and a crowd of the Leicesters break through. I pick myself up. The Boche is moving slowly, and wheezing feebly. He is done for all right. We are in a small glade with broken trees and a barricade of branches and bays before us. The splutter of machine-guns is all about us. This wood is stiff with them! [10]

A detachment of 7/Leicesters remained under Second Lieutenant Evans to hold the left section of Forest Trench whilst, at 4.20 am, Captain Clarke, commanding, with very few officers and the remainder of the battalion, continued forward towards the 'one hour line'. They kept pace with 6/Leicesters to the right without trouble, but the left of their line came under machine gun and sniper fire near an observation post situated some twenty feet off the ground in a tree by the tramway. They suffered sudden and severe losses and were temporarily halted. Captain Clarke and Lieutenant Wakeford were hit, and evacuated during the ensuing

Lt Edward Kingsley Wakeford, 7/Leicesters. Killed by sniper's bullet during the advance through the wood 14 July. Flatiron Copse Cemetery

The remains of the observation/sniping post in Bazentin Le Petit Wood.

exchanges of fire. Being then without officers, Sergeant Walker of A Company, and Lance Sergeant Sherlock of C Company rallied the men, reorganised the line, and moved forward again towards their next objective. Eyre once more:

The Leicesters are moving to our left and behind us. The noise is terrific, a blend of crashes, bursts, and occasionally falling branches and huge bits of trees. We are now drunk with it all and have become utterly reckless. With cries and whoops we dash on again. There's more open space here and we can see the railway line winding like a snake through the trees with a line of sand bags and tree branches flung down just beyond from which the Boche is firing away. The ground is an absolute confusion of pits, holes, ditches, broken gear, and God knows how many dead men.

At 4.25 am B Company of 8/Leicesters crossed the open ground from the north edge of Mametz Wood and on to Forest Trench in support of 7/Leicesters, then moved forward to reinforce the assaulting line. With the aid of two platoons of the supporting 8/Leicesters the line was extended at about 5.20 am to again cover the west side of the wood and to continue the painfully slow progress to the 'two hour line'.

Again the barrage eased forward and, replenishing their belts from the many German stick bombs lying about, Eyre and the bombers gather themselves for their final assault.

By now we are only concerned with getting to that railway line, and are deaf and blind to everything else. Bang! Bang! Bang! Our artillery slams again beyond the railway line, and with a last rush we forge ahead, running and zigzagging like mad under a terrific hail of machine-gun-fire, scramble on to the twisted and broken rails and sleepers and start slinging grenades as fast as we can over the barricade. The Leicesters arrive in small groups and line the barricade, firing over and through the gaps, Lewis guns begin to chatter, and gradually the Boche fire dies down.

Things have quieted down for the minute here. Farther on our fellows are working through the wood. I carefully raise my head above the parapet of the barricade. A welter of tumbled bags and shell-holes, a bit of a clearing and more thick woods beyond. Crowds of dead Germans, some wounded moaning in the open, waving arms feebly. We can't help them though, until the attack goes farther. [10]

The few remaining raiders would now be near the main intersection of the rides running through the wood. From the original party of five, only two bombers, Eyre and O'Donnell remained.

Keeping direction through the ravaged tangle of branches, crushed undergrowth and tree trunks; amidst shellfire and the crackle and spit of bullets was extremely difficult, and parts of the line, in advancing too far, entered the unmarked barrage area and suffered casualties. On the left of the 7/Leicesters front some of D Company came again under very heavy machine gun fire and were pinned down. The men were directed by Lance Corporal Bush to move to their right to skirt the line of fire, but in doing so they became disorientated and lost direction, eventually arriving amongst 6/Leicesters on the right flank of the wood.

The supporting A Company of 8/Leicesters arrived at Forest Trench about 4.40 am, just after the main body of 6/Leicesters had moved on, having just endured a strafing and many losses in crossing No Man's Land. Immediately after, the opportunity for revenge was exploited to the full as on the right flank many German soldiers, fleeing from Bazentin le Grand Wood ahead of the advance of the 2/Border, were killed, caught in the rifle and Lewis gun fire from the east facing defensive flank established by a company of 6/Leicesters to prevent retreating Germans from entering Bazentin le Petit Wood.

The progress of the advance slackened as 6/ Leicesters right flank became exposed. The 7th Division troops had not yet progressed into the village, prompting a request to Brigade HQ, timed at 4.55 am, for reinforcements for that flank. At 5.20 am, having delayed forward movement to await the appearance of the 7th Division troops, the battalion could wait no longer and advanced to the 'two hour' line, mindful of the exposure of their right flank. At the 'two hour line', along the southern edge of the clearing, they were joined by B Company, plus one platoon of A Company, of 9/Leicesters under the command of Captain Anderson, who arrived at about 6.00 am after a forty minute march from their reserve positions in the north of Mametz Wood

Contalmaison Villa photographed on 28 June 1916.

At the south west corner of Bazentin le Petit Wood 8/Leicesters made contact with a patrol from the 1st Division, who had just secured Contalmaison Villa and Lower Wood. But by 4.25 am the leading platoons, having already suffered crippling casualties in attempting to guard the left flank of the 7/Leicesters advance, had been further hit by an attack using both

109

machine gun fire and rifle grenades. The remaining Company (C) was called up to reinforce the left flank, also suffering casualties crossing No Man's Land from the same machine guns that had caused problems to the earlier waves, the injured falling amongst their dead and crippled comrades. C Company continued forward, flanking 7/Leicesters up the west side of the wood from Aston Trench, until progress was eventually arrested by ferocious counter fire about a hundred yards short of the north west corner.

Just before 5 am the commanding officer and the adjutant, arrived at the newly established 8/Leicesters Battalion HQ in the south west corner of the wood, and set out almost at once to investigate an enemy bomb and rifle grenade attack against the recently secured positions in Villa and Aston trenches. The attackers were driven back by determined bombing parties from C Company under Second Lieutenant Alexander, but both he and the much respected commanding officer, Lieutenant-Colonel Mignon, were killed during this action whilst leading the counter assaults. Rifle grenade fire continued to bombard these trenches throughout the morning.

By 5.30 am two Stokes mortars of 110 Trench Mortar battery were in position covering Aston Trench, and a section of the 110 Machine Gun Company moved into the wood.

At about 6 am the remaining three platoons of A Company of 9/Leicesters moved up from Mametz Wood with orders to hold and consolidate Forest Trench, and two platoons of C Company were detailed to carry bombs and SAA to the forward assault wave positions. Lieutenant de Lisle described what happened in his diary

We moved off in artillery formation. The Huns were unceasingly shelling all our approaches heavily...The ground we stood on was literally ploughed up, and deep shell holes were sunk about everywhere...We traversed the old Bosche front line. Here we saw a heap of dead, resting in every possible grotesque position on or near the flattened out trench, quite beyond recognition; a heap of discarded rifles, all twisted and torn by shellfire and by the violence of the fighting; a heap of battered in dugouts, in all forms of disrepair; and finally, a most vivid picture of war was now visible – a machine-gun still pointing towards our lines with the Hun gunner still grasping, in the rigours of death, the traversing handle of the gun when a well aimed British bullet had laid him stark and stiff.

Our task was to fight an unseen enemy in the thickest wood possible, at close range – an enemy well armed with a new

Here we saw a heap of dead, resting in every possible grotesque position.

> *automatic rifle, capable of holding in its magazine 25 rounds, together with numerous machine-guns.*[8]

Dick Read and a colleague were at this time engaged in carrying boxes of SAA hung on a fir pole from 8/Leicesters company dump to their assaulting D Company,

> *Heavy firing and bombing was in progress in front and in the direction of the village, Just then a young subaltern whose name I forget, came along and made us dump our box of S.A.A., 'Just what they wanted. Get some more as quickly as you can. The Boche will probably counter-attack in a few minutes!' he shouted. A gust of shrapnel swept down the trench, killing two men outright and hitting the lieutenant in the shoulder and leg.*[7]

Moving forward with 9/Leicesters' Battalion HQ some three hours later BQMS Bacon commented:

> *A stretch of open country, divided the two Woods, and the German front line of that morning lay roughly 100 yards in front of Bazentin Wood. This open country was ploughed up as efficiently as any ploughed field in England – not a blade of grass was to be seen – nothing but shell holes and they were very deep and overlapping. It was hard work to proceed; the ground was soft and many of the holes several feet deep. Strewn before the German line were heaps of tangled barbed wire, which though so chewed up as to form little means of defence, was*

sufficient to cause trouble and delay to the troops. The trench itself was levelled, but the dug outs had not suffered; the latter, some 40 feet below the ground level, were truly works of art, being fitted with every modern convenience including electric light, and each had at least two entrances. Later in the day, 3 or 4 of the dug outs were utilised as forward Brigade Headquarters.[2]

At 6.00 am dispositions according to 110 Brigade diary were as follows:

6/Leicesters and 7/Leicesters (each less three platoons), with one company 8/Leicesters and five platoons 9/Leicesters form the assaulting wave. Two platoons 6/Leicesters and two platoons 7/Leicesters in Forest Trench, two companies 8/Leicesters forming a defensive flank on left, three platoons 9/Leicesters en route to Forest Trench, two platoons 9/Leicesters carrying (ammunition), and remainder of 9/Leicesters and 1/East Yorks in reserve South East corner Mametz Wood. 110/Machine Gun Company, one section Forest Trench, two Sections Quadrangle Support Trench, and one section Wood Support Trench. 110/Trench Mortar Battery, 2 guns in South West corner of Bazentin le Petit Wood, 2 guns in Mametz Wood, 2 guns South of Mametz Wood, 2 guns out of action.

With the left of the 7th Division still held up by strong opposition and not yet able to advance on into the village, the now intermixed formation of the Leicestershire Brigade stormed Bazentin le Petit from the west at 6.05 am, and fought through to secure the northern part of the village by 6.30 am. 200 prisoners, including three officers, were awaiting escorts back to the compound when, at approximately 6.40 am, the 2/R.I.R. arrived, and the Leicesters handed over that portion of the village to the east of the road

Having returned to the forward battalion dump amidst the cacophony of explosions and bullets, and collected more ammunition and water in red petrol cans, Dick Read recounts:

On the way we went by the aid post [at the north of Mametz Wood]. *Around the Red Cross flag and completely in the open, although shadowed by the trees, three doctors worked amongst the dozens of stretchers lying around, and at several trestle tables.*

Recrossing the old No Man's Land, and reaching Bazentin le Petit Wood near the south west corner, a shell splinter struck and punctured one of the cans, and, Read continues,

We continued forwards in a kind of stupor. We found the numbers of men holding this flank sadly depleted, although by this time they had dug deeply into the bank. I remember calling to the first one I saw sitting in his excavation, his rifle and bayonet held as though he was just getting up. As there was no reply, I looked again. He was dead, and there was a round hole in the top of his hat.

Tin hat with bullet hole – found on 8/Leicesters front 84 years later.

Other men there sampled the water from the cans, which had been manhandled across amidst such danger and difficulty, and declared them petrol-tainted and undrinkable.

Throwing down the other tin, we trudged on to the centre of the wood as previously and, finding the trench deserted except for the corpses, we went forwards towards Bazentin le Petit village where heavy fighting was obviously in progress.

The trees echoed to the constant rattle of rifle and machine-gun fire, punctuated by frequent explosions of grenades in the direction of the village. The shelling had slackened, probably because neither side knew where their opponents were with any accuracy. For a time it had been clear that communications had broken down completely, the signallers either casualties or attempting to repair lines. Casualties among the company and HQ runners had been very heavy; they were sent out and did not return. In short, definite information was very hard to get, and rumour was rife.[7]

Just after 6.15 am the intermixed Leicestershire Brigade assault wave in the wood advanced slowly from the 'two hour' line towards their final objectives, hampered by the broken terrain, the tangles of shattered trees, and continued sniping from all directions.

In the wood near the village the ammunition carriers were fired at from behind. On hurriedly diving for cover and looking back, they spotted a sniper sitting in a tree, having turned his attention towards two men of 7/Leicesters shepherding a line of prisoners, who were stumbling forwards with hands clasped over their heads. Dick Read says,

We spotted our man in the same instant, and, having had ample time to aim, we both fired. The German toppled over backwards and fell to the ground, his steel helmet following his descent through the branches. We both rushed to the spot as one does after potting a rabbit. He was quite dead.[7]

Near the outskirts of the village Read and his colleague dumped their load of SAA with the CSM of A Company 8/Leicesters, all their officers being casualties by that time, and were told that some members of their C Company were nearby, and that B Company were on the edge of and fighting to capture the village, whilst beyond them were the intermixed other battalions of the Leicestershire Brigade.

On the lifting of the barrage an assault party in 7/Leicesters sector, lead by Sergeant Walker, stormed the trench near the northern edge of the wood. Caught between the assailants and the barrage now raging just behind them, the German occupants offered little resistance and about 50 surrendered.

By 6.45 am the line was established along the tramway and eastwards across the north edge of Bazentin le Petit Wood. Officers arriving with the supporting company of 8/Leicesters assumed command and at once set about consolidating the positions. Second Lieutenant Evans with his troops, on the orders of Captain Gwyther, now commanding 8/Leicesters, moved up from Forest Trench with orders to establish a strong point by the tramway, but coming under murderous machine gun fire from the emplacement in the German strong point just outside the wood near the tramway, quickly changed his position to seek cover. Forward progress to secure the road running from the north of Bazentin le Petit to the tramway was impossible.

On the right, in 6/Leicesters sector, having cleared remaining pockets of opposition from the area west of the road through Bazentin le Petit, work began on establishing a defence line, entrenching where necessary and creating strong posts, running from the northern end of the village, thence southwards to the north east corner of the wood, to join 7/Leicesters at the northern edge of the wood, where their positions were exposed to very intense fire.

These exchanges were to prove the start of an increasingly difficult struggle to wrest the north west corner of the wood from well entrenched and determined defenders under orders to hold position at all costs. The machine gun positions in the fortified German strong point outside the wood were to prove problematic throughout the day, causing excessive casualties, and great consternation to the Brigade. 9/Leicesters recorded many casualties including all their company officers during their advance to the north of the wood and village and whilst they were digging in.

110 Brigade situation report at 8.00 am stated that –

The brigade was in occupation of, and was consolidating, the line from the Northern end of the Village, thence along a fence due South to the North East corner of Wood, along the Northern edge of Wood to about 50 yd from North West corner where a line of defence crossed to the western edge, thence along the western edge to South West corner. Attempts to occupy the road running from S.8.a.8.6 to S.8.a.1.3½ [Bazentin north to Contalmaison Villa] *had failed owing to heavy enfilade fire from the left which caused many casualties.*

Just after 8 am, 98/Field Company RE moved up to work, for most of the day under bombardment, in Flatiron Trench, where they constructed strong points and deepened the communication trenches, suffering losses of 23 killed, wounded, and missing.

At 8.15 am Lieutenant Colonel C.H. Haig, commanding officer of 9/Leicesters, with D Company and the remaining two platoons of C Company, moved to Brigade HQ which had been relocated in a German bunker in Forest Trench in Bazentin le Petit Wood. He had orders to undertake the defence of the west edge and north west of the wood. The two platoons of C Company stayed in Forest Trench, and D Company, under Lieutenant Nolan, carried on forward, under orders to clear the north west segment of the wood, and to dig in on the edge.

Fierce fighting ensued and, though repeated forays were made into the area and relentless pressure was sustained throughout the rest of the morning, the German defenders held their positions and remained in control. Lieutenant Nolan was killed in the action, and Lieutenant de Lisle and Lieutenant Smith were both seriously wounded.

Lieutenant de Lisle with his company had advanced first to the south edge of the clearing and, after a patrol forward had determined their whereabouts, were in the process of joining 6/Leicesters line at the north east corner of the wood when they were diverted westwards to help clear the north west part of the wood which had been repossessed by the German counter-attackers. De Lisle wrote in his diary,

The Germans had just counter-attacked in sectional rushes over the open, one section advancing whilst the other gave covering fire. We had done our best to hold them up with rapid fire and machine-guns. But there being no troops on the left forward edge of the wood, the Huns had succeeded in gaining a footing in the wood, 100 to 200 yards or thereabouts – impossible to state exactly. We were ordered to get the company along to the west side of the wood and found the position absolutely untenable, being enfiladed from the top of the wood...The company was much reduced in numbers to about half its original strength, which we formed up along the road [ride] again, in squads of six, at 10 yards interval, under an NCO or the oldest soldier. We found about half a company of E/Yorks and absorbed them into our line.

About forty yards along this road beyond the (west) edge of the wood (about S.7.a.5.0.) was the entrance to a large 40 foot dug-out. We sent a few bombers down to see if it was occupied. Shortly afterwards, 30 Hun prisoners trooped out like a flock of cowed sheep. We had quite a number of wounded with no stretcher-bearers, so we made these prisoners carry our wounded to the rear in waterproof sheets or improvised stretchers, the less seriously wounded acted as escort with rifle and bayonet.

This east-west ride is about 200 yards from the north edge of the wood. The plan was to move forward and to drive out the opposing troops before them:

Just as we were about to go forward, a heavy rapid fire opened on us. Our squads of six quickly disappeared into a prone, extended firing line, and a heavy answering fire opened by us as we lay upon the ground. This went on for about five minutes and then died down as it had arisen.

An improvised stretcher. Prisoners carrying a wounded soldier from Bazentin, 16 July 1916.

On the order to 'Charge!' the line advanced for about ten yards before halting to reply to the

> murderous hail of bullets from unseen rifles. Once more we crawl forwards but only for a few dozen yards, where we man an evacuated trench, and wait for the next burst of murderous fire.

The fire is answered, and the pattern repeated, until the ground to within about a hundred yards from the north edge of the wood is again captured and reoccupied. Rising to urge the remaining men to stop blind fire, and to advance with bombs and bayonet, Lieutenant de Lisle was hit

> I get up to urge the men to stop firing; but almost as soon as I do so I receive a bullet in my neck at close range. It penetrated deep, and the blood gushed out. I fell downwards into a shell hole. One of the men quickly applied my first field dressings as tightly as possible to try to stop the bleeding, for it was bleeding fast. In fact I thought my number was up it bled so hard. The firing was now growing heavier every minute, and the excitement of the moment was great, for we were almost on top of the Huns. I was doing my best to pull myself together, when another officer of our battalion came up from the rear and took over the command.[8]

At about 8.30 am a counter attack aimed at the north of Bazentin le Petit village forced the depleted 2/RIR holding the line there to withdraw south eastwards towards the Cemetery. The Leicesters held on to the northern edge of the wood, and extended and held their line straight into the village on their right, across the north edge of the clearing. During the next forty-five minutes, sustained concentrated rifle fire arrested any further progress southwards by the invaders. Upon arrival of 7th Division reinforcements at about 9.15 am, the northern part of the village was reclaimed, the remaining intruders escaping back towards their line. 6/Leicesters re-assumed their

The ride running north-west from the intersection in Bazentin le Petit Wood. The centre of fierce close fighting throughout the 14th. Note the rising ground. The 9/Leicesters and 1/East Yorks fought bomb and bayonet rushes across this ground.

previous defence line to link with the 7th Division troops at the northern crossroads.

Maintaining the line near the tramway towards the north edge of the wood became more and more difficult under increasingly impassioned pressure from the defenders, and at 9.30 am urgent reinforcements were summoned.

A concerted counter-attack was launched, with a German barrage, aimed at interrupting the forward movement of support troops, falling behind the advance line. An outbreak of concentrated machine-gun and rifle fire preceded a charge against the British at the barricade. Eyre was one of those holding the line:

The Boche machine-guns blaze away furiously, and then from the depths of the wood emerges a surging mob of big, hefty-looking Huns, yelling like souls of the damned and rushing forward with fixed bayonets. Rapid Fire!!! The Lewis guns are blazing away madly. We work our bolts frantically. Germans go down in heaps. We are chucking bombs frantically. Men are going down. Huns appear, scrambling over the obstacle and jumping in amongst us. Faces and huge grey uniforms appear before me through the eddies of smoke. I strike out and lunge. I reel, stumble, and fall amongst a heap of writhing figures. For an instant that seems a lifetime I look up with wide terrified eyes at a gigantic, steel-helmeted, red-faced Hun plunging at me with a bayonet. I await, with terror-stricken soul, for the stroke that will send me to oblivion, when there is a flurry, a figure hurls itself like a battering-ram at the Hun. A terrible yell goes up, and my assailant disappears in a shower of blood and crashes down

Germans rush through the smoke and hail of bullets in a counter-attack on the British positions.

against the sandbags clutching his stomach, with heels drumming and kicking at me.

A rush of khaki figures suddenly appear from nowhere, roaring and stabbing at the Huns. I find myself on top of the barricade, yelling inanely, amid a roar of Lewis gunfire, while the survivors run off falling and stumbling, leaving a trail of dead and moaning figures behind them in the open.

Another forceful attack by the Germans against the north edge of the wood started shortly after 10 o clock. Fierce and sustained fighting followed, inflicting heavy losses on both sides. A and B Companies of 1/East Yorks under Captain Hawkesworth, had been quick to arrive from their reserve position in Mametz Wood to support 7/Leicesters and forced the attackers to retire under the increased rifle and Lewis gun fire.

After the action of 1 July at Fricourt, during which the battalion lost 460 officers and men, 1/East Yorks had spent the period from 5 to 12 July recovering and reorganising at Ville. Once they had absorbed a miscellany of replacements the Battalion was advised of their imminent attachment to 110 Brigade, and moved back to Fricourt (Rose Cottage) at 10.30 pm on the 13th. After the shortest of breaks, they proceeded directly to their reserve position in Mametz Wood from which they entered the battle.

110 Brigade War Diary records the dispositions at 11.00.am as being as follows:

Village of Bazentin, and East portion and Northern edge of Wood. 6/Leicesters, 7/Leicesters – four platoons, 8/Leicesters - 2 platoons, 9/Leicesters – five platoons.

West portion of Bazentin le Petit Wood. 7/Leicesters – eight platoons, 8/Leicesters – three platoons, 110 MG Coy – one section.

In operations against North west corner and north edge of Wood. 7/Leicesters – four platoons, 9/Leicesters – four platoons, 1/East Yorks – eight platoons.

West edge Bazentin le Petit Wood. 8/Leicesters – eight platoons.

Forest Trench. 8/Leicesters – three platoons, 9/Leicesters - two platoons, 110 Trench Mortar Bty 2 guns.

Flat Iron Trench. 9/Leicesters – three platoons, plus two platoons 9/Leicesters carrying.

Mametz Wood. 1/East Yorks – eight platoons, 110/MG Coy - 3 sections, 110/TM Bty – 4 guns.

21st Division HQ was so concerned with the fragility of the situation in the north and north west of the wood, that at 10.40 am 110 Brigade was authorised to use, if needed, a further battalion of 62 Brigade (10

Prisoners from the Bazentin battle marching to Fricourt, 14 July 1916...

Yorks). The plan to attack with two companies from 1st Division westwards from Bazentin le Petit Wood and to use 110 Brigade troops to assist was cancelled due to the continuing difficulty in securing the north west of the wood, and the dismay and increasing frustration resulted in a forceful message from Corps to 21st Division HQ that the situation be resolved and without further delay.

Just before midday D Company of 9/Leicesters trapped and captured Lieutenant Colonel Kumme, officer commanding the Lehr Regiment (3rd Guards Division), two staff officers, and thirty other ranks, in a bunker in the wood. The previous day the colonel had issued orders advising the relief of the 2nd and 3rd Battalions of the Lehr Regiment, and instructing their withdrawal to Flers for regrouping and reconstruction, and to incorporate reserve troops. His order carried on to say, *I will remain in Bazentin le Petit and continue the fight.*

About midday, with all lines being very heavy shelled, a follow up German counter attack was anticipated against the northern sector. The three platoons of A Company, 9/Leicesters, who had spent the morning consolidating Flatiron Trench, moved to Forest Trench and at 1 pm two of the three platoons were sent to reinforce 6/Leicesters' positions in the east of the wood and the village, and the other to the north west to reinforce 7/Leicesters. Captain Boucher (A Company) was badly wounded during this move and died some days later.

The few remaining bombers assembled at the barricade fronting the railway line to await further orders. Eyre could afford to reflect on the battle

New troops are constantly coming up, jumping over us and

...being searched...

> *plunging into the wood, from whence comes the clatter and*
> *stutter of machine-guns and the dull thuds of bomb explosions.*
> *Everything seems unreal – just like a dream. Streams of*
> *prisoners are being collected and sent off under escort. Most of*
> *them, although grimed and blackened by battle, bloodshot of eye,*
> *tattered and torn, look well set up, nothing like the figures of fun*
> *of the comic papers. They have fought hard and well, and the tale*
> *that they must be driven into action at the pistol point is just*
> *moonshine. The Leicesters have been cut to ribbons, and the*
> *survivors of our attacking waves now lining the railway are but*
> *a pitiful reminder of that unfortunate battalion.*

Sometime shortly after midday the surviving attached bombers from 3
Brigade were instructed to return to the rear.

> *The whole area here was a vast charnel house. Amongst the*
> *trees festoons of barbed wire blocking our way, shell-holes, piles*
> *of dead in all attitudes, overturned machine-guns with their dead*

...and secure in the compound.

German crews around them. A dead Boche hanging on a tree branch. Evidently a sniper shot at his post...Lines of men laden with water, ammunition, sand-bags, boxes of bombs, and barbed-wire rolls were coming up at a quick pace, eager to get ahead and get the job over. [10]

Of the fifteen bombers sent in to augment the attacking force, only the sergeant and four men survived. Private Rodwell's body was found at the barricade, and was there buried. Eyre and O'Donnell rejoined 2/KRRC at Becourt Wood that same evening, but were destined to return to Bazentin Wood on the 18th when their battalion came up into the line. Such had been the devastation and carnage that, upon their return, Bazentin was likened to an 'open cemetery leading to the kingdom of Hell!'

The struggle continued in the north west corner throughout the afternoon with the enemy resisting doggedly all attempts to remove them, whilst the northern edge of the wood, which had been under intermittent shelling by 150 mm and 77 mm howitzers throughout the morning, was subjected to an increasingly heavy bombardment, and throughout the afternoon barrages were laid across the southern fringes of the wood and No Man's Land.

At about one o clock another assault party of 7/Leicesters and 9/Leicesters, under orders to clear the north west corner, whilst forcing a way through the thicket of bushes and broken trees, was cut down at close range and wiped out by a machine gun operating from the trench located some thirty yards north of the wood.

During the afternoon a number of attempts by the German forces were made to regain lost ground and to prevent any further advance by the British. As well as the bloody stalemate locking attackers and defenders together in the north west

122

of Bazentin le Petit Wood, determined counter attacks were pitched against the north of the village and the north east of the wood, and against the eastern flanks from the direction of High Wood.

The ammunition parties, including Read, continued their dangerous journeys carrying supplies forward.

> *Two RAMC stretcher-bearers with a wounded officer passed us, one calling out 'The Prince of Wales is just up there'. Sure enough, about two hundred yards further on we came upon a slight figure at the side of the track, red tabbed and tin hatted, holding a long stave on which he leaned as he surveyed the scene around.*[7]

Having delivered another load, Read and his party struggled back through a concentration of tear gas across the broken ground and obstacles of No Man's Land, whilst supporting a man hit in both legs

Awaiting further action. An advanced dressing station stretchers stacked. Note belts of machine gun ammunition in the foreground.

who complained bitterly about his rough journey. On reaching the comparative calm of Mametz Wood, and pausing to rest for a moment, a hoarse cry from the undergrowth prompted them to investigate:

Wiping our eyes and goggles, we peered into the undergrowth and saw a khaki sleeve and outstretched arm a few yards away, moving feebly. Pushing our way in, we found a Welshman of the 38th Division who had obviously been lying out for some days, although he was too far gone to tell us. Kneeling by him we saw that both of his legs were shattered and he was now unconscious.[7]

A quick run to the nearby first aid post summoned the RAMC who prompty attended the two wounded, and stretchered them away.

After stumbling two miles back to the dressing station, crossing back over a No Man's Land under constant bombardment, Lieutenant de Lisle described the scene:

There were more German prisoners carrying our wounded to the rear than we had men of our own. These same men a few hours before were thirsting for our blood. Perhaps they were now; but fate had so disposed of them that they could not refuse to do all in their power for the wounded; otherwise the vigilant British sentry would let them know of it in a way never to be forgotten.[8]

The situation in the north west corner remaining unsatisfactory, C and D Companies of 1/East Yorks were called up and reported to Lieutenant Colonel Challoner of 6/Leicesters, and their Battalion HQ was relocated in Bazentin le Petit Wood. C Company moved to the north east corner of the wood without opposition, and D Company to the north edge, 10/Yorks moved up to reserve in the south east of Mametz Wood and, in addition, although not called, 1/Lincolns (62 Brigade) were made available if needed.

The events surrounding the severe attack against the north of the village and the north east of the wood which started in earnest at about 2.30 pm are confused by conflicting accounts in the war diaries of the battalions involved. The 2/RIR account differs from that of 6/Leicesters, and 1/East Yorks, and a later exchange of information between the CO of the supporting 2/Gordons, sent to assist in repelling the attack, and Brigade HQ seems largely to corroborate the Leicesters' information. The situation must have been chaotic to say the least. A heavy bombardment which wrecked the trench line hurriedly dug at the north of the wood, killing many, must certainly have forced a relocation of the line and, accurate reporting being

A refreshing cuppa for the walking wounded from Bazentin. 63 Field Ambulance in attendance, 17 July 1916.

absent due to the lack of officers, the probability seems the Leicesters' line was re-established across the clearing due west of the church. However the diary of 6/Leicesters, albeit completed later, states that the counter attack was stopped by Lewis gun and rifle fire at the road running from the north west corner of the village to the tramway and that positions were held through the day. This report may be accurate for the positions on the north edge of the wood, but certainly a substantial intrusion was made by the counter attackers into the north east of the wood and into the village; although the line was certainly re established immediately on the withdrawal of the attackers.

110 Brigade diary states,

> *3.00 to 4.00 pm. Enemy counter attack against the North of Village and Wood was repulsed with heavy casualties to both sides. British artillery fire accidentally directed short, added to the German artillery barrage directed at the north edge of wood, causing much consternation, and many injuries. Shrapnel directed at retreating German troops inflicted severe casualties.*

Whilst this combat was being fought, further efforts to remove the German forces from the north west segment of the wood continued with renewed desperation. At about 3 pm the Brigade Commander, Brigadier-General Hessey, arrived to direct operations personally against the stubborn defence, ordering every available man to attack.

Lieutenant Colonel Haig, Captain Emmett and Second Lieutenant Stephens, all of 9/Leicesters, with about 50 Leicesters and a further 100 1/East Yorks formed an assault party. Haig with the 1/East Yorks and some 9/Leicesters fought north and eastwards sweeping towards the tramway, but they were halted by enfilade machine gun fire about the tramway. Second Lieutenant Stephens was hit and killed at this point. Bacon recorded,

> *The enemy fired promiscuously with machine guns and trench mortars from three directions, the din was awful, bullets whistled and cracked at all elevations and angles, one had literally to crawl or lie on the ground to avoid them. Our positions were about twenty yards from the enemy. At a given signal rapid fire was directed on the enemy for two minutes and then a charge was ordered; every man who got up was knocked down, wounded or killed immediately. Some minutes later this was repeated with the same result; it was Hellish – the men dropped like stricken sheep. The enemy were not in large force but were well concealed behind the brushwood and a bank, and well supplied with machine guns which they used to devastating effect. Finding that it was impossible to take the positions by a frontal attack, it was then decided that stealth would have to be employed. To this end certain of the men were ordered to crawl within a few yards of the enemy and then rush him; this succeeded where bolder methods failed, but our casualties were exceedingly heavy. After hand to hand fighting for some thirty minutes and suffering severe loss, the position was captured together with many*

The position of the German fortification north west of Bazentin le Petit wood from where terrible casualties were inflicted on the British.

> *machine guns, while such of the Bosche as were able, retired to a trench some fifty yards in front of the wood... It was decided to dig in just within the wood.*[3]

The north west of the wood was finally cleared by this painfully slow but relentless close range and costly action sometime before 6.30 pm; strong posts were then created on the north and north west edges of the wood, and were manned and consolidated during the evening, patrols repeatedly combing the north west sector throughout the night.

Forty men with Captain Emmett, having fought through to the north west edge of the wood, shot dead four German observers, and then just after 7 pm, attempted a charge against the trench some forty yards distant. Captain Emmett and thirty-six of the men were cut down and killed by machine gun fire.

An attempt to recover Captain Emmett and his party was caught in heavy sniper fire; Lieutenant Hinckley was wounded and most of his men killed or wounded. Sniper fire from these enemy trenches just north of the wood, fire from the machine gun emplacement in the strong point some 200 yards beyond the wood near the tramway, and enemy shelling of the northern sector continued into the night, but no further counter attacks materialised. 2/Gordons arrived early in the evening to greatly ease and improve the situation on the right of the Leicesters' line. This has been covered in the account of the 7th Division in the preceding chapter.

At 7.30 pm 110 Brigade received a further insistent order from Corps HQ to occupy the road running from the north end of the village to the tramway.

Meanwhile, throughout the day the Royal Engineers field companies with attached pioneer companies of 14/Northumberland Fusiliers had worked on the battlefield. 126/Field Company RE interrupted their construction of strong points to help fight off counter attacks, and 97/Field Company RE worked on restoring the tramway to a useable state.

The night of 14/15 July passed fairly quietly. Bazentin le Petit Wood

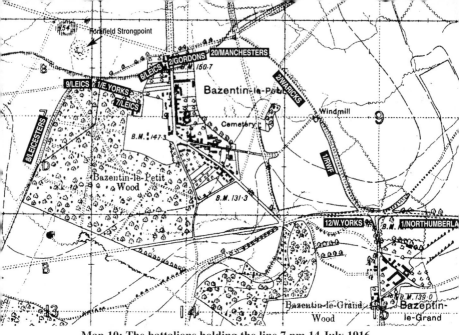

Map 10: The battalions holding the line 7 pm 14 July 1916.

was shelled intermittently, the north west corner receiving most
attention, and occasional sweeps of machine gun fire pelted the
occupants. The shelling, the mess of shattered trees, shell holes, and
tangled branches, slowed considerably the flow of rations and supplies,
but consolidation work on the northern extremities and in the wood
continued without respite. Bacon commented on the tragedy around
him:

> *One of the greatest difficulties was that of evacuating the
> wounded...casualties had been heavy and dead and wounded
> were lying about in pitiful profusion all over the Wood. The
> nearest Field Ambulance Post was in Mametz Wood, and all but
> the walking wounded, needed to be carried the considerable
> distance under the most difficult of conditions...Moreover the
> Brigade had been so reduced in strength that only a few could be
> spared for stretcher bearing, and even then it was a very long
> and tiring stumble with a loaded stretcher. Many of the wounded
> had perforce to lay in the Wood with little or no attention for
> thirty or forty hours, and this in may cases cost the man the loss
> of a limb and in some cases his life. Some of the wounds were
> ghastly to look upon, and it was indeed a cruel and never to be
> forgotten sight, and there was always the chance of the wounded
> being again hit, for the enemy never ceased to shell the Wood or
> the open country behind...in later battles the arrangements for*

the evacuation of the wounded were much improved, but on this occasion at least they were very ineffectual.

Our aeroplanes had been particularly active throughout the day, flying low over the enemy and firing drum after drum of machine gun bullets into him, though be it said that his aircraft though active, caused us little trouble and none of his kite balloons could be seen in opposition to some thirty or forty of our own.[3]

Around 9.00 pm the remaining able bodied soldiers of the intermixed battalions on 7/Leicesters front were reorganised, and manned the trench line throughout the quiet night.

When they arrived back at HQ, by now mud-stained, unshaven, with grimy faces, and bloodshot eyes, Dick Read and the other ammunition carriers were instructed by RSM Cattell of the Leicesters to take a

Leicesters and prisoner. Note battle order with fixed bayonet and wire cutters attached.

In Happy Valley – British and German walking wounded head towards Mametz, 17 July 1916.

break, but to be ready to act as runners. In fact one more journey was to made before dark, after which, over tea, bully-beef, and biscuit, they ruminated over the days events:

This set us running through the names of our mates we knew already to be killed, wounded, or missing. Both of us had lost all our best pals, we sat there with leaden hearts, lost in our thoughts. Eventually Jackie broke the silence. 'Plenty of rations

Pushing across muddy ground between Bazentin and Mametz. An engineer is assisted by a prisoner, 17 July 1916.

'There'll be hell to play'. A few of the Leicesters dead 14-17 July 1916.

Sgt Ernest Knott

Sgt Harry Shillaker

Pte Frederick Webb

Pte Leonard Evans

2/Lt Arthur Howard

Lt. G.T.L. Ellwood

Pte Frederick Robinson

Pte William Henry

Pte Fred Barker

Pte Horace Lefevre Phillips

tonight, Dick!' nodding towards the pile, 'Enough for the whole battalion, eh? About six times too many.' He added bitterly, 'Christ, there'll be hell to play in Leicester and Loughborough ...and Coalville...and Melton ...and Uppingham...when they know about this. The Leicester Brigade, eh? Bloody well wiped out!' And he trailed off into silence again, immersed in his thoughts.[7]

The day's action had accounted for most of the battalion officers of 7/Leicesters. Lieutenant Wakeford, and Second Lieutenants Pickering-Clarke, Simpson, and Reed, were all killed in action in the wood. Lieutenant Colonel Drysdale had been wounded before the battalion reached Mametz Wood, and Captain Clarke, Lieutenant Houghton, and Second Lieutenants Thomson, Orrit-Nichol, and Webb, during the action of the day.

Five hundred and thirty five men were dead, wounded, or missing. 6/Leicesters had suffered seven officers killed and twenty wounded, and five hundred men killed, wounded or missing.

The following letter was sent by CSM Stafford on 21 August 1916 to relate to the wounded Captain Ward (8/Leicesters), recuperating in England, his account of the battle and news concerning other members of the company. D Company covered the left flank of the 110 Brigade successfully, but at great cost, attacking in the opening wave the Villa and Aston Trenches under machine-gun fire from the direction of Contalmaison Villa. The companies then extended the flank cover, working northwards along the west side of Bazentin le Petit Wood.

The letter is reproduced in its entirety.

Second Lieutenant Frank Farmer Hind 6/Leicesters attached to 110 Trench Mortar Bty. Killed at Bazentin, buried at Flatiron Copse.

Sir,

Mr Goodliffe has today shown me parts of a letter you have written to him. He suggested that I should write to you and give you as many details of the Battle as I possibly can. First of all, Sir, I remember you lying there wounded with a man holding you up. You were shouting to the Company to go on, and I took up the cry also. They who were not hit 'carried on', but how anyone reached the German trench I do not know. I am pleased to say, Sir, what remained of the Company got into the right trench. One party about a dozen lost their direction a little and were making for the Bazentin Wood, they, however were redirected and recovered the proper direction.

We did not catch it from the front but from the left flank. The enemy seemed to have collected on the left of that communication trench and treated us severely with liquid fire, bombs, and their devilish machine-guns. When we eventually reached their lines most of 'em retired to the left [our left, their right]. I sent as many men as I could spare to clear that trench which they did remarkably well. We had no trouble from that quarter the whole of the four days we were in. Their dugouts were packed and no man escaped from them whilst we were in. They were all well bombed and the only retaliation they made in the trench from a dugout was one bomb, which did not reach the top of the steps, but made myself and L/Sgt Hills A.E. jump. We had no more trouble from that quarter.

'D' Company took one prisoner, which we had to, as both of his legs were broken and was absolutely helpless. We blocked the junction of their fire trench and the communication trench in no time, and every man set to work and we soon had some fire steps made and the trench deepened. On the right of the Company the enemy attempted to force their way into the trench luckily after we had had a breather, and it was there that the Colonel was killed. We had a job to keep up with them in bombs, but we all had the bombs collected from the casualties in front and the German bombs came in handy too. L/Cpl Mason fought well in this defensive action but was unfortunately killed. We were shelled fairly heavily too, on occasions, and suffered a few more casualties. We were in the trenches four days and every man

breathed a sigh of relief when we marched through Mametz Wood for the last time

The Company suffered heavily, Sir, 4 Officers (2 killed, Messrs Greenaway and Bowells) 2 wounded, you and Lt. Ewen, and 130 other ranks. There were no Sergts killed, Sgt. Kirk was very badly wounded but is in England now. Sgts Buxton, Croker, Hills, were wounded badly before we reached our objective. Sgt Reed of the Lewis Gunners was killed on the last day in the trench. L/Sgt. Hills was wounded by shrapnel a day or two after the attack. Cpl Rayson, L/Cpls Rogers, Wheeler, Morley G. Holyoak, Mason,E., Dunn, West, Chesham, and Clarke were all killed , Sir.

Unfortunately, Sir, the boys had no opportunity of showing the ability with the Bayonet. The Bayonet work was done in Bazentin Wood which we missed. L/Cpl Clarke A.A. showed great pluck, Sir, I believe he was the first man over, but was killed by a rifle bullet. Our Lewis Gunners suffered heavily, Sir, only about three or four getting through. In one sense, Sir, the Company was lucky to have had one left.

Personally, Sir, I was extremely lucky, bullets pieced my clothing and equipment in six places and a bomb dropped at my feet but I jumped out of the way and caught a tiny bit on the cheek, the force knocked me over though.

I think, Sir, you have every reason to be a proud man (I hope you will pardon me saying so). Only well trained and well disciplined troops could have faced the Hell we faced. It was your training, Sir, and I'm a proud man to have served under such an Officer. The 'Boys' did wonderfully well, Sir, and I'm proud to be Com Sgt Major over the 'Remnants'. We have always prided ourselves on being the BEST Company in the battalion, and I think Bazentin le Petit proved it.

My ambition is, Sir, to bring the Company up to its old efficiency. It is our duty in remembrance of our late C.O. and you, Sir, who made the Company what it was.

I hope, Sir, you will soon be in good fettle again, I hope your wounds will heal quickly and with as little pain as possible. I'm not going to wish you a speedy return to the front, Sir, as I would be wishing you no good. With every wish for a speedy recovery from everyone in 'D' Company. I know the boys would want me to include their good wishes.

I remain, Sir, Your sincere Sergeant, Ben. W. Stafford, Coy. Sgt. Major 'D'Company.[4]

Chapter Eight

THE DAY'S EVENTS OF 14 JULY SUMMARISED

Before 10.00 am on 14 July almost all opposition had been overcome on the 3rd Division front and on the 7th Division front to their immediate left. The 21st Division was still fighting hard for the north west corner of Bazentin le Petit Wood and, although the northern sector of the wood and village, and the north east, would be severely counter-attacked later in the day, at that time the corn covered slopes north east of the villages up to High Wood appeared empty of enemy activity. Several senior officers, including Brigadier-General HC Potter (9 Brigade) and Lieutenant-Colonel CA Elliott (C.R.E. 3rd Division), walked up the slope to reconnoitre High Wood; they saw neither enemy troops nor defences, and drew no fire.

Major-General Watts, commanding 7th Division, proposed using his reserve 91 Brigade to occupy High Wood, but was told to wait for the cavalry, and Major-General Haldane, commanding 3rd Division, proposed using his reserve 76 Brigade to pursue the enemy, but was instructed to continue to hold the brigade in reserve in case of counter attack.

The Official History says:

> It was in the highest degree unfortunate that, at a moment when fresh troops were at hand to maintain the impetus of the advance, such a delay should have been imposed by higher authority. Responsibility might well have been delegated to the divisional commanders, both experienced and capable leaders, who were in the best position to know what could, and what could not, be done. There was no lack of troops to cope with any unforeseen emergency, for the head of the 33rd Division had already reached Montauban. Obviously the infantry should have

The corn covered slopes appeared empty of activity. Up the slope – Bazentin le Petit to High Wood.

been encouraged to exploit its success to the utmost, since the more progress it made through the German defences the more favourable would be the conditions for the cavalry when, and if, mounted troops were able to come through. Every hour was precious. At this juncture it might have been possible - at least the attempt was worth making - not only to occupy High Wood, but to take up and hold a position in its vicinity along the ridge, which would threaten the envelopment of Poziéres on the left and Delville Wood, on the right. Yet High Wood was not to pass completely into British hands until after two whole months of bitter and costly fighting.

Orders to the divisional commanders stated that the objectives were to be secured and the positions held with no further advances. A number of reasons have been proposed for lack of immediate action in exploiting the unexpected opportunity: that the use of cavalry was politically favoured by High Command; that the risk of exposing flanks, both east and west, to enemy action would have been too high; that the salient so created would have been untenable. The substantial width of the front which was available for occupation by available reserves, seems to render these reasons as excuses. The capture of High Wood and the Switch Line was the ultimate objective of the battle plan.

In hindsight it would appear that further incisive action at this juncture would have capitalised on the advances of the New Army battalions early in the day, and justified more the bloody losses they incurred in securing their objectives. The hours lost at this stage certainly enabled the Germans to launch counter-attacks and to bring up reinforcements, however jumbled, to arrive in time to repulse effectively efforts to occupy the German Switch Line positions in High Wood, and thereby nullify the immediate threat to the enemy eastwards to Delville Wood, westwards to Poziéres, and northwards towards Martinpuich. Perhaps the success of the advance had overtaken the competence of the Corps Command to react, and the brief time slot of opportunity passed uncapitalised.

Fierce fighting continued throughout the day in Longueval and along the edge of Delville Wood. As a result of the continuing attempts to secure the north west corner of Bazentin le Petit Wood by the 21st Division, whose forward positions were now under heavy enemy artillery fire and the number of battlefit combatants diminishing, the joint attack by the combined 21st and 1st Divisions was first postponed from the originally planned time of 2.30 pm, to 4.30 pm; and after the heavy counter attack by the German forces against the northernmost allied positions in the village, the offensive was cancelled.

A report received at 3.10 pm by XV Corps HQ stating (incorrectly) that the whole of Longueval was now in allied hands, prompted Lieutenant-General Horne to issue orders at 3.30 pm that the 7th Division would advance upon High Wood at 5.15 pm.

It was not until after 5.00 pm that Brigadier-General Minshull-Ford, commanding 91 Brigade (7th Division), received these orders. His brigade, which was to be supported on the left by the leading brigade of the 33rd Division, was ordered to be in deployment position on the right of Bazentin le Petit cemetery and ready to move forward at 6.15 pm, when a planned barrage by the field artillery was due to be lifted. Arrival on station by the appointed time from their position east of Mametz Wood was impossible – the leading 91 Brigade battalions – 1/South Staffordshire and 2/Queen's arrived at about 6.45 pm.

The orders called for cavalry cover on the right flank but Brigadier-General Gregory commanding the cavalry assembled south of Montauban did not receive the orders advising him to move his Brigade up to the region of Sabot Copse until 5.40 pm. His mounted troops did well to arrive in the valley between Caterpillar Wood and Bazentin le Grand Wood at 6.25 pm. Upon arrival the line of command transferred from XIII to XV Corps, and the leading cavalry squadrons proceeded immediately to their appointed deployment positions on the right of 91 Brigade troops.

Although an artillery barrage was spectacularly expended an hour early, at 7 pm on 14 July, 1/South Staffs and 2/Queen's with 20/Deccan Horse and 7/Dragoon Guards covering their right, began the advance from the newly won British positions in the valley west of Bazentin le Petit cemetery towards the green mass of High Wood standing on the ridge some 1200 yards up the slope, as yet undamaged by shellfire. The 33rd Division arriving from reserve had failed to receive the orders and, as a result, no cover was provided on the left flank of 1/South Staffs.

At 7.30 pm, Brigadier-General AWF Baird, commanding 100 Brigade (33rd Division), on learning from the 91 Brigade headquarters that support was expected, on his own initiative ordered 1/9 Highland Light Infantry (Glasgow Highlanders) and 1/Queen's to occupy the void between High Wood and Bazentin le Petit.

The advancing cavalry came under rifle fire from enemy outposts hidden in the untended and overgrown crops near High Wood, and from a machine gun post in Delville Wood which was disabled from the air. After action against positions in High Wood during which further losses were incurred, by 9.30 pm and in the fading light a defensive line was established from the southern corner of High Wood to adjoin the British line west of Longueval. This had entailed the removal of German machine gun and rifle outposts, assisted by fire from the Lewis guns situated at the windmill.

Lyn Macdonald in her excellent book on the Battle of the Somme recounts an experience of Second Lieutenant FW Beadle R.A. 159 Brigade (33 Division), who, in the late afternoon of 14 July as Forward Observation Officer for the divisional artillery which was reassembling in the area of Caterpillar Valley, had moved via the road intersection north of Bazentin le Grand to reconnoitre the ground and, with the aid of an accompanying signaller, to relay information to allow accurate range and directional fixing for the barrage which was to precede the next assault against High Wood and Switch Line. However in the chaotic mess of churned up trenches and shell holes, instead of moving north eastwards towards the forward observation post near the windmill, they inadvertently headed up the old German communication trench to within 300 yards of High Wood. Lieutenant Beadle recalled:

> *I had no idea we were so near the Germans, but the mass of trenches there were so involved that we had the utmost difficulty*

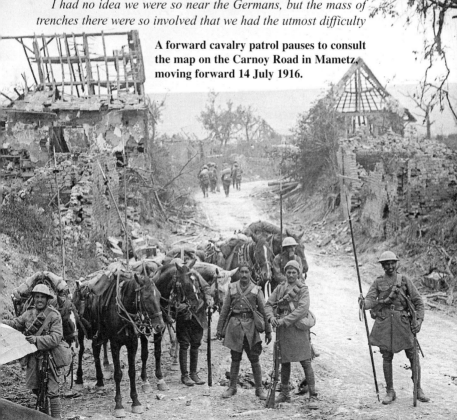

A forward cavalry patrol pauses to consult the map on the Carnoy Road in Mametz, moving forward 14 July 1916.

and really were simply taking a chance. There was a terrific noise going on with shellfire and it seemed extraordinary to me that this trench was more or less abandoned. We were being very cautious as we went and I had my revolver at the ready – ready for trouble! Then, as we turned the corner of one of the traverses of the trench, there, approaching me, was a German soldier armed with a rifle. The extraordinary thing was that he had his rifle slung on his shoulder and the other odd thing was that he was wearing an overcoat and this was July, although it had been showery. He saw me at exactly the same time as I saw him and he raised his rifle, but he must have been impeded by this overcoat because he couldn't get it up to his shoulder quick enough. I knew jolly well that if he had I should have caught it. It was either him or me.

It was the first time I had fired my revolver in anger, so to

speak. The first time I'd ever seen a German soldier, apart from prisoners. I killed him with one shot. I felt nothing. All I felt was relief. I knew I had no option, but I didn't stop to think of the morality. It was either him or me. Afterwards, I often wondered who he was and where he'd come from and whether he was married and whether he had any family. I've thought about that very often but, at the time, I didn't think of anything except where on earth were we, and where on earth was the infantry we were supposed to contact?

Lieutenant Beadle was in the prime position at 7 pm to witness the charge of the cavalry against High Wood.

It was an incredible sight, an unbelievable sight, they galloped up with their lances and with pennants flying, up the slope to High Wood and straight into it. Of course they were falling all the way because the infantry were attacking on the other side of the valley furthest away from us, and the cavalry were attacking

Indian Cavalry gather in Caterpillar Valley 14 July 1916, before the attack on High Wood.

very near to where we were. So the German machine-guns were going for the infantry and the shells were falling all over the place. I've never seen anything like it! They simply galloped on through all that and horses and men dropping on the ground, with no hope against the machine-guns because the Germans up on the ridge were firing down the valley where the soldiers were. It was an absolute rout. A magnificent sight. Tragic.[9]

During the engagement the cavalry suffered 10 dead, 91 wounded and three missing, and 43 horses killed and 103 wounded.

The infantry met with little resistance and, although 1/South Staffs on the left were harassed by machine gun fire from high ground in the direction of Martinpuich they, together with 2/Queen's, entered High Wood to form a defensive line along the eastern edge and across the middle. 1/3 Durham Field Company RE followed to construct strong-points and consolidate the positions, and frequently joined the infantry in actions to thwart frequent counterattacks. Reinforcements having arrived during the afternoon, the enemy was again in strong possession of the Switch Line trench and the western side of High Wood.

The Official History summarised the situation:

At 9.45 p m on 14 July General Rawlinson issued an order for the resumption of operations next morning: the successes gained were to be exploited, and the capture of the previous day's objectives completed, full advantage being taken of the confusion and demoralisation of the enemy: the cavalry divisions were to remain in their bivouacs ready for action. By the morning of the 15th however, the Germans, with reinforcements continuing to arrive, had sufficiently recovered to oppose stoutly every new advance on the front of the Fourth Army, although their plan to counter attack and regain the line Longueval – Bazentin le Petit miscarried.

British supremacy in the air was not to be challenged seriously for some time to come; but weather conditions began to handicap the offensive by hindering aeroplane observation of artillery fire. The 15th July was misty and over cast until the evening; persistent rain set in on the afternoons of the two succeeding days, making the movement difficult over the heavy ground.

The German official history states that the British, by their surprise attack at dawn, 'evidently meant to smash a way through'. Other accounts claim that complete surprise was not achieved, and that the first onslaught only penetrated at a few points; but the parties which did get in, worked right and left,

Thistle Dump Cemetery with the dark mass of Mametz Wood in the background. The cavalry brigade charged from left to right up the slope.

rolling up the defence, 'which they had not done on 1st July'. The struggle was a severe one, and very heavy losses were sustained; among the captured were the commanders and staff of the Lehr Regiment and the 16th Bavarian Regiment and of the 1/91st Reserve and III/16th Bavarians. On this day, the 16th Bavarians, which had all its three battalions in the front line, lost nearly 2,300 officers and men. (Official History)

During the day, 42 German officers (including 2 regimental commanders and staff) and 1400 men had been taken prisoner. The German forces suffered very heavy losses; however, contrary to regimental reports, the official history notes,

Far more execution could have been done had the infantry made better musketry practice on the retiring enemy; in many units the men, owing to lack of training, could not be depended upon to hit anything even at 300 yards; in despair, officers took up rifles and picked off fleeing Germans until the machine guns could be brought forward.

No clue is recorded as to the identity of the alleged offenders. The following letter, for communication to all, was from the Commander in Chief and dated 15 July

The attack carried out so successfully by the Fourth Army yesterday reflects the highest credit on the Commanders and Staffs who planned and arranged it and on the troops of all ranks who executed it with such vigour and bravery.

It was a very fine feat of arms and has opened the way to further successes.

I congratulate you and all under your command very warmly not only on what you have already achieved but on the vigorous efforts being made to the utmost at the very favourable opportunities opened up by your success.

So ended the eventful day of 14 July, the first, and the decisive day, of the Battle of Bazentin Ridge. During the battle 9194 officers and men were posted as killed, wounded or missing in the assault across the whole ridge. The struggle for Longueval and Delville Wood on the right of the battlefront developed into a protracted action, continuing until 3rd September 1916, and is officially recorded as The Battle of Delville Wood.

Chapter Nine

THE BATTLE CONTINUES: 15-17 JULY 1916

On receiving confirmation of the successful achievement of the objectives, a message from Fourth Army HQ was telephoned by their liaison officer, Captain Serot, to the French XX Corps HQ saying, 'Ils ont osé; Ils ont reussi' – 'They dared, they have succeeded'. General Balfourier replied, ' Alors, le general Montgomery ne mange pas son chapeau!' – 'Then, General Montgomery doesn't have to eat his hat!' Undoubtedly this was a fittingly understated retort to Montgomery's remark of the previous evening concerning the consumption of hats in case of failure, unexpectedly relayed by Captain Spears to the General.

Although the majority of the military objectives for 14 July had been realised, Contalmaison Villa, Bazentin le Petit village and wood, Bazentin le Grand village and wood all captured and consolidated, and Trones Wood on the extreme right flank had been occupied and an east facing defensive front established, fierce fighting continued in Longueval and along the edge of Delville Wood. Here II/16 Bavarians were reinforced by II/26 Regiment (from the German 7th Division) and a battalion of the 99th Reserve Regiment. The battle for Delville Wood would only start in earnest on 15 July and not be concluded until 3 September.

During the night of 14/15 July the newly won ground occupied by the 3rd and 7th Divisions remained quiet. The 21st Division, having finally, and at great cost, overcome the enemy and occupied the north west of Bazentin le Petit Wood during the evening of the 14th, were not further engaged until later in the morning of the 15 July.

The German official papers recorded,

The appearance of cavalry near High Wood gave rise to alarmist reports at Corps and Army headquarters that 'the British had broken through northwards between Longueval and Poziéres and by 9.40 p m.(8.40 p.m. British time) had reached the line Flers – High Wood – Martinpuich and were still advancing.' At night, therefore, (General von) Below placed all reserves, 8th Division (Armin's IV Corps), 5th Division from the general reserve at St. Quentin, 24th Reserve Division, now beginning to enter the line south of Longueval, and 8th Bavarian Reserve Division south of Peronne – under Armin, who was given orders to bring to a standstill the British who had broken through, and to counter-attack as soon as the situation allowed. Before anything could be done the true state of affairs was ascertained, and Below then gave instructions that a big counter-stroke need not be attempted: and he brought the 5th Division, and the 8th Bavarian Reserve Division back into general reserve.

Although in the early hours of 15 July General Sixt von Armin was still doubtful as to how far the British advance had penetrated, he had determined upon a counter-attack by the 8th Division of his IV Corps. Orders for the counter-attack, which was to be supported by the field artilleries of the 8th, 7th, and 3rd (Guard) Divisions, were issued at 2 a m on 15 July. The 72nd and 93rd Regiments were to move against the line, W.N.W. corner of Longueval – north-west corner of Bazentin le Petit, and each put two battalions in front. The men were tired, after much marching, and the advance was made in the darkness under heavy artillery fire. On the right the II./93rd Battalion deployed south of Martinpuich soon after 4 a m and got in touch with the troops holding the Switch Line. The III./93rd arrived at the Switch Line west of High Wood about the same time. The III.172nd had reached a sunken road north-east of High Wood, whilst the II./72nd arrived at the Switch Line east of the wood. One company of the latter pushed on and occupied a part of the

Building the dugouts, Bazentin le Petit.

front line north-west of Longueval. 'Owing to the tremendous
effect of the British artillery and the activity of the British
airmen, it was impossible for the attacking battalions to advance
by daylight. They sought cover in portions of the trenches and
shell-holes by sections and platoons.'

At 5.30 a m. Armin wanted the troops to make a fresh effort,
as he considered the situation critical, but a further advance was
impossible: the British artillery fire was too formidable, and
units in the battle front were so mixed that difficulties of
command were very great. Moreover, the artillery was not ready.

Commencing at 3.40 am in the mist of the morning of 15 July, the
cavalry squadrons were withdrawn without further loss from their
overnight positions between Longueval and High Wood. Five days
would elapse before any attempt would be made to advance east
towards Delville Wood from these positions.

On the evening of 14 July the arrival in the western edge of
Bazentin le Petit Wood of 1/Loyal North Lancs (2 Brigade, 1st
Division) was covered by 7/Leicesters. At 9 am on the 15th 1/Loyal
North Lancs attacked westwards and gained about 400 yards along the
German second line trench (Villa Trench), and about 200 yards of the
support trench (Aston Trench), before progress was halted by a
combination of a wrecked and rain soaked trench system and accurate
machine gun fire.

However, at 5 pm further progress was attempted by 2/Welch (3
Brigade) who were initially trapped by the machine gun fire but, after
the onset of darkness, renewed efforts proved successful, and during
the night a further 600 yards of trench system was captured by
bombing parties. Fortified posts were established adjoining with 34th
Division troops who, following the lifts of a divisional artillery barrage
launched from Caterpillar Valley, had fought north westwards across
difficult and wet terrain towards Poziéres during the night.

Rifleman Jack Brown MM, A Company 16/KRRC (100 Brigade),
whose battalion moved up ready to enter the fray on the 15th against
the Switch Line, sheltered overnight in Bazentin le Petit Wood. He
recalled the march forward past Mametz Wood and the disturbing
scenes which assailed his senses.

We was going to High Wood. That's what we was told. It was
a hot day and the stench was something awful. The guns were
there firing and all the artillery blokes had got their shirts off.
There was two banks, one on either side of the road, about chest
high – if you could call it a road! And when we actually looked,

they weren't banks at all. They were heaps of overturned wagons, dead horses, broken equipment, and not to tell a lie, dead bodies as well. The smell was terrible. We went up to a place and, believe it or not, they called it Happy Valley! On the way up there was a trench at right angles to where we was, and it was full of dead Germans, just standing there where they'd been shot. You could see their heads and shoulders, just stood up where they'd been firing from. They hadn't fallen down and they'd gone as black as pitch.[9]

On 14 July 21/Manchesters had been brought up to reinforce 2/Queen's and 1/South Staffs (91 Brigade) in High Wood and had held their positions overnight. During the 15th several attempts were made to clear the German forces from the remainder.

At 9 am the troops of 91 Brigade moved forward from their positions towards the Switch Line running through High Wood, the first of a number of attempts to advance repulsed with much machine gun fire and dogged resistance, a pattern repeated throughout the day.

Around 2.30 pm an enemy counter-attack followed a heavy barrage on the southern part of High Wood. At 4.45 pm a replying artillery barrage was followed by a further British attempt to regain ground, but heavy and persistent German bombardments on the rear, cutting signal wires and hindering communications, and then more German counter-attacks, confused the situation further until at 11.25 pm Lieutenant-General Horne ordered a complete withdrawal of 91 Brigade during the night of the 15th /16th, leaving the wood to be kept under constant fire by the divisional artillery. The German II/165th (7th Division) and the III/72nd (8th Division) followed up and reoccupied the whole of the wood.

On 15 July, whilst 91 Brigade was unsuccessfully attempting to progress in High Wood, the 33rd Division (Major-General HJS.Landon) made an attempt to storm the Switch Line west of the wood. 98 Brigade and 100 Brigade moved in a north westerly direction towards Martinpuich, from their positions covering a front from the north west corner of Bazentin le Petit village to the western corner of High Wood. 1/9 Highland Light Infantry covered the High Wood end of the line, and although they had needed to send three platoons to engage the enemy in the western side of the wood during the previous night, no contact had been established with the 91 Brigade troops on their right. 1/Queen's formed the centre of the assault line, with 1/9 HLI on their right, and 1/Middlesex (98 Brigade) having arrived during the night, on their left. In the late morning of the 15th the Germans counter-attacked the north west of Bazentin le Petit Wood and after a short and fierce engagement, were eventually repelled, but not before causing great concern to Brigade HQs.

The 21st Division, although counter attacked and constantly under

Troops outside their dugouts 16 July 1916. Looking south-west from Bazentin le Petit Village.

fire from the fortified strong point to the north west of Bazentin le Petit Wood, held their line and covered the left flank. At 9 am on the 15th, after an ineffectual but spectacular thirty minute barrage, and at precisely the same time as 91 Brigade in High Wood began their attack,

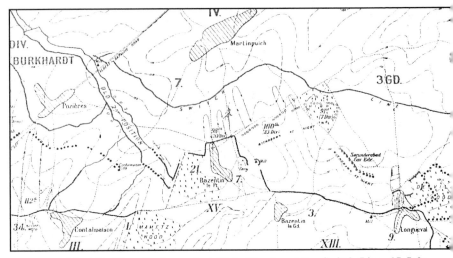

Map 11: The attacks against High Wood and the Switch Line, 15 July 1916.

the formation rose to attack up the slope to the Switch Line trench.

The advancing forces were almost immediately cut by enfilade fire, machine gun posts spraying crossfire from the direction of High Wood and from the position north west of Bazentin le Petit Wood, as well as strafing fire from Switch Line emplacements. After gallant but hopeless repeated attempts to reach the German trenches, in spite of being reinforced by 16/KRRC (Church Lads Brigade) and 2/Worcesters, and with losses escalating, all attempts at forward movement were abandoned. By 5 pm the survivors were back where they had started the attack

Corporal Jack Beament MM, A Company 16/KRRC, recalls the 15 July attack against the German positions in High Wood.

> It was a horrible, terrible massacre. We'd lost all the officers out of our company. We lost all the sergeants, all the full corporals, and all the NCO's right down to Herbert King who was the senior Lance Corporal. He was my pal and he brought A Company out of the wood. He rallied them and brought them out. There were more than two hundred of us went in. And Herbert brought them out. Sixty seven men. That was all.[9]

By 8 am on 16 July the withdrawn 91 Brigade was bivouaced behind Bazentin le Grand; 100 Brigade was withdrawn to the east of Bazentin le Petit, near the windmill. The 21st Division handed over to the 33rd Division and was withdrawn to reserve on 17 July; and the 7th Division took over from the 3rd Division part of the front east of Bazentin le Grand.

148

Chapter Ten

THE BATTLE CONTINUES 21st DIVISION
15-17 JULY

Orders for the 16th July, issued by the Fourth Army at 11.58 pm on the 15th, had directed the XV Corps to secure and consolidate the whole of High Wood, and announced a simultaneous attack by all three corps for the 17th: the XIII Corps on Guillemont and Ginchy; the XV Corps on the Switch Line between High Wood and Martinpuich; and the III Corps on the German defence further to the west, including Poziéres. The French Sixth Army and the Reserve Army would co-operate on either flank, whilst the 1st and 3rd Cavalry Divisions and the 2nd Indian Cavalry Division were to remain in their bivouacs ready to move at two hours notice.

At 9.30 am on the 16th, however, the commanders of the III Corps and XV Corps, with their chief artillery officers, attended a conference at army headquarters, when it was decided that High Wood should be included in the objectives of the main operation, now fixed for the 18th July. There could, indeed, be little doubt that no important success was now to be won except by means of another properly mounted attack upon a broad front....General Rawlinson was well aware that the time needed for adequate preparation would be utilised to the full by the Germans in bringing up reinforcements and in strengthening their line, but he hoped that, meanwhile, they might be induced to spend their strength in counter-attacks with which he would be able to deal. (Official History)

Corps orders were that the attack against the Switch Line was to continue on 15 July, by the 33rd Division against the line running south west from High Wood, whilst the 1st Division fought westwards towards Poziéres along the Villa Trench line. The 21st Division was to fill any gaps arising between these two divisions, and the reserve 64 Brigade was instructed to be positioned south of Mametz Wood before 8 am; ready to move up through Bazentin le Petit Wood as and when required.

Of 7/Leicesters, only 100 men answered the morning roll call. These were regrouped and spread along a 150 yard front guarding the north edge of the wood. Very early in the morning of 15 July, as a result of what could have been a disastrous mistake in reading orders, by whom unspecified, 110 Brigade were ordered to withdraw to the south east of Mametz Wood. The exhausted troops, eager for respite, did not hesitate in complying and started their withdrawal without delay, leaving the seconded 1/East Yorks guarding the wood, just one company the west edge, and the rest the whole of the north and north west.

As soon as the mistake was realised, the retiring troops were intercepted and turned back with frantic haste to their original positions where, by 10.45 am, after much cursing, they were all finally, and fortunately, reinstalled, although totally exhausted. The account by 9/Leicesters differs somewhat, in that their diary records that at 2 am the battalion received orders to withdraw to the centre of Mametz Wood, and arrived there at the appointed time of 8 am, but that at 9 am they were ordered to return with all haste to their original posts. The differences could be due to the orders having reached the battalions spread through the wood at different times, but only fortuitous circumstances prevented a major incursion by the opposing Germans.

4.5" Howitzers moving up past Mametz Wood 15 July, 1916.

Bacon summarised the feeling of the men:

> During the attack of the previous evening to secure the north west segment the brigadier had promised that the brigade would be relieved the following morning in the event of its capturing its objective. One whole day and night in the battle was sufficient to exhaust the stoutest, and the men were tired, hungry, and beginning to become fed up, and the numerical strength being so reduced, our defence against an energetic enemy counter attack appeared doubtful. Having to go back into the old positions after what was generally thought to be a relief lowered the men's spirits to Zero, and even then the relief was expected hourly.[3]

The roll call of 9/Leicesters whilst at Mametz Wood was answered by only 120, but, in spite of the doubts, the German counter attack which followed their return was repulsed, and forty of the attackers were captured including six officers.

Captain Kelly's recollection of the incident was as follows;

> ...as the result of an unfortunate misunderstanding the Brigade were ordered to withdraw, though, in fact, there was no one at hand yet to relieve them. I was standing in Mametz Wood when the Brigade Major called to me to collect everyone in sight, and take them to the front line, while he himself seizing a horse from a gunner, rode round sending back the battalions. I got together about eighty men, joining them onto the returning battalions then, wandering round Bazentin le Petit Wood, found the Brigadier sitting in a shell hole, meditating gloomily over the risk which had been incurred.He gave me a note for General Headlam, commanding the 64 Brigade, who we understood to have his headquarters in Bazentin village on our right. On reaching the village I found it empty and being heavily shelled, so, after trying the cellars turned south and eventually found General Headlam in a shell hole. Villages made easy locations on the map and were usually death traps; for the former reason they were often laid down in orders as headquarters for brigades or battalions, and for the latter reason as often the headquarters found shell holes in the neighbourhood to be more congenial.[6]

Throughout the day Bazentin le Petit Wood was heavily shelled, and a barrage rained on the area between there and Mametz Wood. At 11.00 am a message from General Hessey, commanding 110 Brigade, reported another heavy attack against the north west corner of Bazentin le Petit Wood and, acting on this information, the commanding officer 62 Brigade requested that 64 Brigade send up a battalion to assist, advising that 62 Brigade were carrying up extra bombs and SAA. This message was noted as misplaced and not received, but 110 Brigade diary records that from 11.00 am 64 Brigade HQ was established in the south east of the Wood and that assistance was available if required.

Forty men of 7/Leicesters arrived in the north west sector of the wood just before 2 pm and, with their assistance, 8/ and 9/Leicesters repelled the German counter-attack which had intruded and which, from a range of a mere 20 yards, was inflicting heavy casualties with bombs and rifle grenades and was forcing back the line.

At 1.30 pm a company of the 10/KOYLI was sent from their position in the south east of the wood to investigate the situation in the north west, but by the time the company arrived the enemy had been driven out. 10/KOYLI War Diary records their success in driving out the intruders! Around midday a Stokes mortar gun was despatched to the north of the wood for use against the strong point, still a painful thorn in the side of the Brigade.

General Headlam, commanding 64 Brigade, who was in Bazentin le Petit village, intended to cover the left flank of the 33 Division advance using 10/KOYLI, but as the Switch Line attacks failed the plan was no longer relevant. From 6.30 pm 64 Brigade was withdrawn to the vicinity of Fricourt, but with one battalion made available to 110 Brigade on demand.

British machine gun fire from strong posts established on the west and north west edges of Bazentin le Petit Wood was effective against German soldiers forced to flee from the communication trenches running north east from Villa and Aston Trenches, ahead of the bombers of 1/Loyal North Lancs.

At 3.20 pm XV Corps ordered (received by 110 Brigade H.Q at 5.30 pm according to their diary) that the road adjoining the north end of Bazentin le Petit Village to the north west corner of the Wood must be cleared, secured and held by the 110 Brigade; and a number of unsuccessful attempts followed.

At 9 pm an attempt by Second Lieutenant Sargeant and 20 men of 9/Leicesters to dig in along the north west edge was foiled when they became isolated by a barrage of rifle grenades fired from the trench just outside the wood and falling behind them. The party was never heard from again, and all were assumed killed. Much bombing, sniping fire and automatic rifle fire continued into the night in the north west sector.

97/Field Company RE and one company of 14/Northumberland

Fusiliers worked all the day consolidating Bazentin le Petit Wood and village, although the planned position strong point No.11 was still in enemy hands and obviously could not be constructed. The engineering work was continued on the 16th by 98/Field Company RE and two companies of 14/Northumberland Fusiliers.

Acting on orders issued by 62 Brigade HQ at 9.30 pm, on the 15th and received by Battalion HQ in Mametz Wood at 11.00 pm on the 15th, Captain Crone and Captain Goater with D and C Companies of 10/Yorks, started an attack at 2.15 am on 16 July, to occupy the road running from the tramline at the north edge of Bazentin le Petit Wood to the north corner of the village, which the 110 Brigade had been unable to secure. After a successful assault, recorded as 'with few casualties', but during which Lieutenant Cornaby and Lieutenant Kinnach were killed, consolidation by a company of 1/East Yorks moving from the right proved impossible, and they were forced out by a torrent of enfilade fire and bombing from their left.

The battalions in the front line, by the evening of the 15th, were short of rations; Bacon describes just how difficult a task this was:

...throughout the day the enemy shelling continued, and his machine guns were very active, continually sweeping through the wood, which prevented one when moving about from assuming an upright position. Dusk came and gradually deepened into night with no signs of relief. By this time all rations and water had been disposed of. Those for the following day were sent up to the rear Brigade Headquarters in Mametz Wood, and there dumped, to be sent for by the men in the line. Few men could be spared to fetch them. Shortly after midnight I was sent forward to the companies to recruit all available men. With great difficulty ten men were got together and a start made. It was daylight when the dump was reached, and after a short rest the return was made, plus one can of water each. At this hour a very thick mist pervaded by tear gas hung in the air, which coupled with the disgusting and rotting stench formed a most ghastly and nauseating alliance. The wood was reached at last, but the only opening could not be found as the fog was so thick as to preclude all but a few yards ahead from view, and we stumbled through the broken and tangled undergrowth, trusting to luck to find the way. Four hours we wandered thus, occasionally stopping for a rest for the water was heavy but too precious to leave, and we dare not turn up without it. Continually we passed the same spot but found no troops except wounded, nor could we find a way out of

the wood, although it was of but small area. Finally stumbling across the railway running through the wood, we managed to find Headquarters. It was now about 11 am and all thought we had been knocked out. Corned beef, biscuits and jam were munched with evident relish by officers and men alike, and had there been more it could easily have been disposed of. [3]

The morning of 16 July started fine with clear skies and sunshine, but as the day progressed increasing cloud brought drizzle and then a night of persistent rain and increasingly wet underfoot conditions.

No. 2 Section 98/Field Company RE, along with two companies of 14/ Northumberland Fusiliers started work at 4 am and continued through until 5.30 pm, completing four strong points in the wood and constructing a new strong point in the village at S.8.a.8.5 (on the west side of the village road some 50 metres before the northern cross roads), which, when completed, would be garrisoned by 9/Leicesters.

In answer to a call at 2 pm on 16 July from 1/East Yorks, who were under heavy fire from the enemy work outside the wood, a platoon of 9/Leicesters lead by Second Lieutenant Lee was redeployed to the north edge arriving at around 3 pm. Whilst en-route they searched but failed to find any remains of the party under Second Lieutenant Sargeant which had disappeared under fire the previous evening.

After enduring a day of strafing fire from the machine guns in the strong fortifications situated to the north west of Bazentin le Petit Wood, Stokes mortars concentrated a bombardment across wide arcs onto the fortifications during the evening, at last quietening the guns, and reducing the danger to the troops guarding the northern boundaries. The heavy enemy shelling of the day continued throughout the night on the wood, the many who were dug in there suffering from 'a new type of gas shell being used'.

Captain Bent, with D and B companies of 9/Leicesters, completed the take over of the west side of the village of Bazentin le Petit at about 7.45 p.m., and garrisoned the newly constructed keep. Captain Bent, as Lieutenant Colonel commanding the Battalion, was destined to be awarded a posthumous Victoria Cross for his gallantry at Polygon Wood in the Ypres Salient the following year.

On the evening of the16th Lieutenant Howarth, with a party of nine sappers of 97/Field Company RE, arrived at the north of Bazentin le Petit Wood with a push pipe, prepared to deliver explosives in an attempt to disable the unassailable strong point some 150 yards ahead; but such was the intensity of the enemy firepower that effective action to dispense the charges was prevented.

Captain Philip Eric Bent.

Careful reconnaissance early in the morning of 17 July revealed that, following the Stokes mortar bombardment of the previous evening and the westwards advance by the 1st Division, the enemy had evacuated during the night the strong point to the north of Bazentin le Petit Wood which had caused such extreme problems. 15/Durham Light Infantry occupied and consolidated the positions and, much to the relief of Brigade and Corps HQs, engineering work fortifying the road from the tramway to the north west corner of Bazentin le Petit, and the establishment of strong point No 11 could at last be completed.

At 1.10 pm on the 16th orders were issued by XV Corps (received by 21st Division HQ sometime after 3 pm, and by the battalions much later – 9/Leicesters diary records receipt at 9 pm) that 64 Brigade was to relieve 110 Brigade during the night of 16/17 July. The relief was completed at 8.30 am on 17 July, and 110 Brigade (with the exception of 1/East Yorks, who remained in their positions and returned to 64 Brigade) withdrew to bivouac in the vicinity of Fricourt Village in the positions vacated by 64 Brigade. 7/Leicesters war diary notes that rain made the under foot conditions treacherous and, under bombardment, the need to wear gas masks added to the difficulties.

Captain DV Kelly, M.C. concludes his account of the Tigers battle at Bazentin:

> *It had been a gruelling experience for the Brigade, which had lost 2000 casualties out of about 3300 effectives. A very large proportion of the casualties were fatal, particularly amongst officers, and of my old battalion (6/Leicesters) most of those I had known best had been killed or badly wounded. Of the others, I grieved particularly over Colonel Mignon of the 8th Battalion; one of the most charming of the many fine men I knew through the War, who was killed while leading a bombing party like a subaltern, and I remember vividly seeing him lying on his back still clutching a rifle.*
>
> *In the later stages of the war commanders of brigades and battalions were constantly being enjoined to stay at their headquarters while a battle was in progress, but during the early Somme battles colonels and brigadiers were, as far as my experience goes, seldom to be found in dugouts.*[6]

Colonel Mignon.

15/Durham Light Infantry, having taken over from the Leicesters, records an anxious night on the 16th/17th being bombarded by *gas shells, tear shells, HE and shrapnel, and all sorts of explosives.* Having been almost continually in action since 1 July, they were exhausted and pleased to hand over their positions to 1/Middlesex on the evening of the 17th.

During the 16th and 17th 126/Field Company RE were busy rebuilding the narrow gauge railway, completing some 1250 yards through Mametz Wood, and then on to Bazentin le Petit Wood.

10/Yorks were engaged in Mametz Wood during 14 to 17 July, clearing the wood, burying the dead, deepening trenches and strengthening strong points, before the battalion was relieved by 9/Highland Light Infantry at 4.30 am on the 18th and was withdrawn to Buire.

The weather of 17 July continued dull and overcast with showers, adding to the complexity of the immediate battle plans.

The position of 64 Brigade at 8.30 am on 17 July was as follows:

10/KOYLI - Bazentin le Petit village and the northern edge of the Wood (having relieved 6/Leicesters);

15/Durham Light Infantry - North west and west edge of the Wood (having relieved 7, 8 and 9/Leicesters);

9/KOYLI - one company in Flatiron Trench and south east of the Wood, the remainder at the south east corner of Mametz Wood;

1/East Yorks - en route to the south east of Mametz Wood returning after secondment to 110 Brigade.

The bombardment of Bazentin le Petit Wood continued throughout the 17th with HE, and at night with more persistent gas shelling.

The 21st Division arrived during the morning of the 17th in the vicinity of Fricourt, F.4.b.2.5 (6/Leicesters arrived 1 am, 8/Leicesters at 8 am).

Bacon reported that

Hot soup, tea and rum was served to the men as they came in,

Motorised and horse drawn ambulances of 63 Field Ambulance RAMC collecting wounded from Mametz village. 17 July 1916.

who although dripping wet and unsheltered from the rain, were glad to lie on the sodden ground and sleep unworried, for the past three days not a wink of sleep had been possible. Stragglers continued to arrive up to 11a.m.[3]

Dick Read was another one who got back to Fricourt:

The Leicestershire Brigade trooped wearily down through Mametz Wood and back to a fairly sheltered spot near Fricourt. I remember seeing our brigadier, Hessey, dirty and bedraggled as the rest of us, walking slowly down the light railway track with the aid of long stick, head bowed like a weary old shepherd. Our acting C and B Company commanders; the one a boyish figure of a subaltern, who had taken over in the heat of the battle from his wounded captain, and who had aged ten years in the last four days; the other, Captain Beardsley, martial yet, although dirty and unkempt, his left hand bandaged. He had gone into action with his sword, and now it was sheathed at his side, but he strode proudly at the head of his remnant – a pitiful few – who followed him like faithful dogs.

We marched off at dusk and left the Somme with very mixed feelings – of sorrow at the thought of those we had left behind, and of individual relief at being out of it, if only for a time.[7]

The day was spent regrouping and resting expecting to return to Bazentin le Petit, but instead the brigade was withdrawn to various billets and bivouacs in Ribemont. Respite would not be too prolonged before their next major involvement at Guedecourt towards the end of September.

110 (Leicestershire) Brigade casualties during the Battle for the

Bazentin Ridge July 12th to July 17th 1916 were:
For example 8/Leicesters lost the following officers:

	Killed or D o W.		Wounded		Missing		Total	
	Officers	ORs	Officers	ORs	Officers	ORs	Officers	ORs.
6th Battalion	5	55	20	362	2	76	27	493
7th Battalion	14	72	6	309	-	147	20	528
8th Battalion	5	66	12	310	-	95	17	471
9th Battalion	8	47	9	294	1	52	18	393
110 M.G.Coy	-	4	5	16	-	4	5	24
110 T.M.Bty	1	1	2	7	-	-	3	8
Total	33	245	54	1298	3	374	90	1917
1/East Yorks	6	30	6	186	-	126	6	348

Killed in action 14th - 17th July 1916
Lt Col JG Mignon, 2/Lt AGE Bowell, 2/Lt FCG Greenaway, 2/Lt J Alexander.
Died of Wounds: 2/Lt J Lea
Wounded: Captains F Ward, CAB Elliott, J Abbott, and JL Warner, Lt NAG Ewen, 2/Lts VHL Davenport, EP Frake-Walters, M Dove, AE Gregory, WS Murphy, WG Jamieson, HR Gross.

Lieutenant Alexander Charles Nicholas de Lisle, 9/Leicesters, an extremely gallant young officer, who had been wounded at Bienvilliers-au-Bois in October 1915, was again seriously wounded and repatriated during the Battle of Bazentin Ridge and, after transferring to the Royal Flying Corps, was killed in 1917 whilst on a flying mission in the Ypres sector. His body is buried at Dozinghem Military Cemetery, Poperinge, Belgium. His diary, which records with a startling and moving enthusiasm the atmosphere before and during the action, was written with the intention of enlightening the public in general as to the way and conditions of the warfare, and concludes:

If munition workers and others engaged in Government work could see for the space of five minutes such veritable cemeteries as Mametz Wood, the Quadrangle, or Bazentin le Petit, they would never dream of resting from their labours for holiday or other purposes till the Huns are beat and humbled to the dust, and the Honour of England vindicated and our glorious Empire triumphant.[8]

Chapter Eleven

THE 7th DIVISION 15-17 JULY 1916

Brigadier-General CJ Deverell in his 20 Brigade report wrote,

I attribute the complete success, combined with comparatively small loss, of this operation to the following causes.

(1) The very thorough artillery preparation on the two days previous to the assault.

(2) The very close co-operation between infantry and artillery during the assault.

(3) The immediate infantry assault as the barrage was lifted in succession.

(4) The skilful leading of all battalion commanders in the concentration marches, and the careful selection of routes to be followed.

(5) The excellent spirit prevailing amongst all ranks. Everyone knew what he had to do and did it.

(6) The insistence of every man digging himself in whenever he was likely to be halted for any prolonged period under shell fire.

(7) The element of surprise which characterised the assault.

(8) At no time was the infantry crowded. For the assault of all three objectives it was not even necessary to use the battalion reserve companies.

(9) The width of the area on which the attack was undertaken.

From the evening of the 15th, 20 Brigade, having handed over their overnight positions to 22 Brigade, were withdrawn to reserve in the following locations...

9/DEVON REGT – CATERPILLAR WOOD (On the night of 15/16 the wood was subjected to heavy gas shell bombardments from 11.30 pm. until 1.00 am and again from 2.15 am until 3.00 am; in the late morning of the 17th the battalion was relocated to WILLOW AVENUE.)

2/BORDER REGT – POMMIERS REDOUBT and POMMIERS TRENCH.

8/DEVON REGT – WHITE TRENCH

2/GORDON HIGHLANDERS – FRICOURT WOOD X.29.c.8.3.

20/M.G. COMPANY – After company reconnaissance, 8 guns

moved on 18th to the vicinity of S16 central, in readiness for sweeping in the direction of FLERS and the SWITCH TRENCH with indirect fire. 8 guns in reserve in MONTAUBAN ALLEY

20/T.M.Battery – BLACK ALLEY

Various reconnaissance duties were carried out but the next 20 Brigade operation would be the attack against High Wood planned, after delays, for 20 July in conjunction with the 33rd Division on their left and the 5th Division on their right.

The War Diary of 9/Devons records one officer and 16 other ranks killed with 94 missing and wounded during the action at Bazentin le Grand.

An addendum from the Commanding Officer, Lieutenant Colonel H Storey, to the G.O.C. 7th Division states,

> *I should like to bring to the notice of the G.O.C. the good work performed by 2nd Lieut. E.B.Green who although only joining the battalion on the 17th July ably commanded his company under difficult and trying circumstances after his C.O. had been killed.*
>
> *Also, No. 6462 L/Cpl Goddard. B. 6/DCLI attached 9th Bn Devonshire Regt. who carried out a valuable reconnaissance, locating hostile machine guns and bringing in wounded under heavy fire.*
>
> *Also Stretcher bearer No. 11817 Pte Wilson G.M. who throughout the night of 12/ 13th July - at period of exceptionally hard work – and under heavy fire, showed the greatest devotion to duty and disregard of danger. It was largely owing to his example that the stretcher bearers did such good work.*

The 24/Manchesters (Pioneers) were busy during the 15th reconstructing forward access ways. Four platoons from B Company spent from 8 am till 6.30 pm repairing the road from S.14.c.3.5 to S.14.b.95.90 (from west of Flatiron Copse to cross roads north of Bazentin le Grand Wood) to enable the artillery easy passage. C Company repaired approaches further back, three platoons between 11 am and 7 pm making good the road laid by the Germans between X.29.b.5.5 and up the valley through X.30.a and S.19.a and S 20.a, and one platoon fixing the route F.5.d.1.9 to F.5.b.3.7. The following days were spent making good on various sites in the Bazentins and Mametz.

The 7th Division Signals Company had established communication, either visual, or telephonic, or both, by the late afternoon of the 15th to all battalions in their relocated positions, in time to summon the commanding officers to Divisional Headquarters, for briefings on the forthcoming rescheduled attack on High Wood and the Switch Line.

After a search on the evening of the 15th for a suitable site, the Signals HQ for the coming battle was established in a large dug out at S.14.b.15.35 (between the Bazentin woods). All equipment and the linemen were transferred to the new location during the 16th but, after postponement for 24 hours and then again indefinitely, on the evening of the 19th instructions were advised to the signals that the attack against the roads from the eastern side of High Wood towards Longueval would commence at 3.35 am on the 20th, and without delay a double cable was reeled out to S.15.a.9.9 (the cross roads north of Bazentin le Grand Wood) ready to service the HQs of the attacking battalions of 20 Brigade.

From the 15 July 2/RIR was relieved by 2/Warwicks and after assembly at the south end of the village, moved to Brigade reserve in Mametz Wood. 2/Warwicks, with four machine guns, deployed B and C Companies to relieve C and D Companies of 20/Manchesters in the north east of Bazentin le Petit village and patrol west, and A and D Companies the cemetery and northwards.

These positions were held, under continual shellfire, until the 16th when 98 Brigade relieved the 22 Brigade in Bazentin le Petit village. 2/Warwicks withdrew to Fritz Trench, until the 19th when two companies returned to trenches in the north east of Bazentin le Petit Wood with the other two companies in support.

The Battalion HQ of 2/RWF moved forwards to an abandoned German artillery dugout in the northern part of Bazentin le Grand Wood, and although counter-attack activity was recorded in the north and north west of Bazentin le Petit on the 15th, in spite of numerous causes for alarm no action took place on the north eastern flank, except for the harassment by constant shellfire.

Robert Graves, at this time a Captain in 2/RWF (33rd Division), had arrived with his battalion at the south of Mametz Wood from the direction of Fricourt on 15 July, in a thick early morning mist contaminated by lachrymatory gas, having been delayed and diverted en route by a German shell barrage. Surrounded and

The Welsh brigade attacks against Mametz Wood. Plaque at the Welsh Dragon Memorial

saddened by the as yet unburied dead of the new army battalions of the Royal Welch and South Wales Borderers who had earlier helped capture the Wood, he recalls having been shocked by dead horses and mules, human corpses being all very well, but that animals being dragged into the war seemed wrong. Large chalked letters 1/RWF on the side of a German gun reminded him of friends in that battalion who were in the close vicinity, including Siegfried Sassoon and Edmund Dadd, and a visit to their lines established that Sassoon was with the transport reserve; but he was able to learn about the exploits of his fellow battalion, and their losses from Dadd.

His battalion remained camped at the south east of Mametz Wood for two days before moving up to the north of Bazentin le Petit Wood, being bombarded during the move with a new type of gas shell and as result losing half a dozen men. Relieving the Tyneside Irish, they held the line adjoining 4/Suffolks facing north west towards the Switch Line Trench and Martinpuich, and helped construct the two cruciform strong points three hundred out into No Man's Land. Visiting during the night the most northerly of these strong points, Robert Graves, whilst walking along the Bazentin to High Wood road in bright moonlight, crossed himself, he recalls, on passing the sinister figure of a short, powerful, and black bearded German sergeant major wearing full pack and lying dead and supine in the middle of the track with arms outstretched. An eerie, ghoulish, and tragic tableau, came into view as a number of Highlanders who, trying to escape from shelling, had huddled head and shoulders into shallow dugouts previously and hurriedly scraped into the left bank of the road and, wounded and kilted had there died, seemingly hiding from the fearful black beard.

From the limber of a German gun team destroyed by shell blast whilst galloping out of Bazentin on the Martinpuich road, Graves recovered a carved lump of chalk, decorated in colour by one of the

The sunken road – Bazentin le Petit to High Wood. Where Robert Graves saw the ghoulish tableau in the moonlight.

dead gunners, and illustrating flags, military mottoes, and battles. This he sent back to the highly respected battalion medical officer, Dr. JC Dunn, who was later to write *The War the Infantry Knew* and who, after the war, retained this memento under a glass dome in his consulting room in Glasgow. [11]

In readiness for the assault on High Wood 2/RWF moved on the 18th to the area between the cross roads north of Bazentin le Grand Wood and the Cemetery.

Also with 2/RWF at the south east corner of Mametz Wood, Captain Dunn noted that to avoid gas shells the bivouac positions needed to be moved forwards some 100 yards ahead against the road (the track which now passes in front of the 38th (Welsh) Division Red Dragon Memorial). Dunn continues,

> *The night [16th] was spent close behind our main artillery position. The noise was more nearly 'ear-splitting' than anything I have known. A battery of French seventy - fives had taken station at dusk just in the rear. Their high-pitched bark repelled sleep, and attracted the German artillery, whose overs reached the Indian Cavalry picketed close by the French guns...All about us the air was heavy with the reek of the dead in Mametz Wood...Throughout the day batteries rolled into Happy Valley, the prosaic called it the Valley of Death, east of Mametz Wood and on to the slight rise of Caterpillar Wood, until these sites were stiff not with guns but with batteries.*
>
> *On 17th the rain, which started on the previous afternoon, and the infernal noise of the guns lasted through the night...There was nothing to do but watch the guns beside us in action and the enemy's counter-battery. Again and again the gunners were driven to cover, and guns were disabled; once the tyre of a wheel went spinning 20 or 30 feet into the air. The German gunners could not have shot better over open sights. There was a story the next day of an observer with signalling gear having been found up a tree in Bazentin Wood.* [13]

On the 18th his battalion relieved the 4/Kings in the line between the cemetery north west of Bazentin le Petit village in position ready for the next attack against High Wood. *After dark, hordes of rats came over D Company's ground. They made a noise like wind through corn. It was uncanny.* The 2/RWF, with Dr. Dunn still as the Medical Officer, would return to the Bazentins again during the final counter offensive in August 1918.

Frank Richards DCM MM, who served on active service

throughout the war, also joined A Company 2/RWF at the south east of Mametz Wood on 15 July.

He wrote a forthright and interesting account chronicling events during his time around the Bazentins. Serving together in the trenches further north, at Hulluch, his fellow signaller and compatriot Private Dann had a haunting experience, petrified when a huge black rat appeared and stared directly at him for some time, remaining fixed in spite of the clods of earth thrown at it by Frank Richards. Shaken beyond reason, Dann gloomily forecast that this was an omen for the worst, a forecast that would be forgotten under the consuming duties of the weeks following. Shortly after arrival at the south east corner of Mametz Wood Richards relates:

> *Enemy shells were now coming over, and a lot of spent machine gun bullets were zipping about. He* [Dann] *sat on the edge of the trench, writing his quick firers* [postcards], *when – zip ! – and he rolled over, clutching his neck. Then a terrified look came on his face as he pointed behind me. I turned and just behind me on the back of the trench saw the huge black rat that we had seen in Hulluch. It was looking straight past me at Dann.*

Completing the quick-firer (pre printed postcard). Reserve dugouts southeast of Mametz Wood, 15 July, 1916.

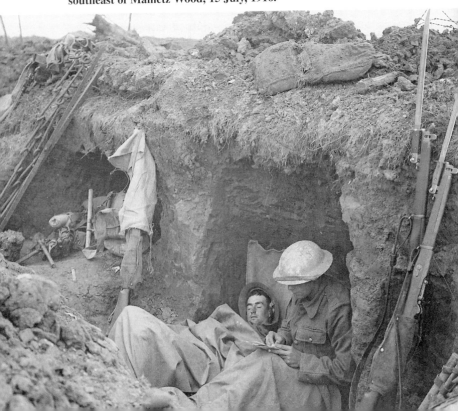

**Caterpillar Valley – Mametz Wood in the background. Towing the 6"
Howitzer is a truck by the American Four Wheel Drive Company of
Cliftonville, Wisconsin, USA. One of 18000 supplied during the war.**

*I was paralysed myself for a moment, and without looking at me
it turned and disappeared in a shell hole behind. I turned round
and instantly flattened myself on the bottom of the trench, a
fraction of a second before a shell burst behind me. I picked
myself up and looked at Dann, but he was dead. And there by his
side was the large rat. I seized hold of its tail and threw it back
in the shell hole it had been blown from. It was the only weird
experience I had during the whole of the War. If I hadn't handled
the rat and flung it away I should have thought that I had been
seeing things.*

Caterpillar Valley and the area was crammed with artillery:

*One afternoon a couple of guns in front of us were blown to
bits and two young artillery officers were led past us, hysterical
and horribly shell-shocked. They were the worst cases I ever saw,
and anyone would have been doing them a kindness if they had
put them out of their misery.* [5]

On the ridge above their position was a battery of small howitzers
which was suddenly caught in a rain of uncannily accurate shell-fire
and destroyed. Shortly afterwards, a man in grey was seen by two
soldiers of 1/Middlesex to enter a dugout in Bazentin le Petit Wood, but
on investigation no trace of anyone was found. Whilst one of them kept
watch, the second reported the incident to an officer who, with the aid
of a torch discovered a concealed door, but justifiably cautious
announced loudly that a mistake must have been made and silently
indicated a re-ascent to the outside. Soon after they had quietly re-
entered the dugout, the door opened and a German officer emerged, to
be disabled by a single shot from the officer's revolver. The secret door
revealed two trench telephones connected by cable to High Wood,
which were being used from the hideout to report positions to the

German artillery. Upon interrogation the captured officer admitted having volunteered for the work, and to being very proud to have been able to serve his country so well.

Communication during this period must have been very frustrating for the combatants. The War Diary of 1/RWF for the 15th records,

> It was however very difficult to find out at any time what was happening on even our immediate flanks; and it is worthy of note that our own H. Qtrs. was for almost the whole period the only means of communication between 91st Brigade H.Qrs and their two advanced Battns – Queens and South Staffs.

On being relieved by 33 Brigade on 16th July, 1/RWF and 2/RIR with Nos. 2 and 4 sections of 22/MGC, withdrew to the Hammerhead in Mametz Wood, where they remained regrouping in readiness for the attacks on the Switch Line and High Wood. No.3 section of 22/MGC

The artillery sergeants mess, ammunition and ration boxes. Mametz Wood 17 July, 1916. Note water cart and spare stretchers. IWM Q 4017

replaced No.4 in the sunken road near the windmill. On the 18th No. 1 section moved into an indirect fire position on the high ground between Bazentin le Grand Wood and Village and, in preparation for the forthcoming action, from this vantage point, starting at 9.30 am and continuing until 5.30 pm, systematically fired bursts at ten minute intervals against the south west face of High Wood, and positions between High Wood and Martinpuich, as well as hourly concentrated fire against the Switch Trench north of High Wood. 10,500 rounds were fired during the day.

Sir Douglas Haig who, according to Lady Haig, regarded the push of 14 July as the army's best day of the war, issued to Fourth Army Headquarters on 16 July a Special Order congratulating all ranks on their 'very fine feat of arms'.

A Special Order was issued by Major General DGM Campbell C.B., commanding 21st Division

I cannot too strongly express to all ranks my intense admiration for their splendid gallantry in actually breaking through the German first and second lines. No Division has a finer performance to its credit.

Until, however, the high ground north of the German second line has been seized and consolidated, we cannot consider our work complete.

Although I fully recognise the tremendous strain which has been imposed on all ranks, I am confident, after their previous magnificent performances, that I can absolutely rely on them to answer any call that may be made upon them until they have wrested their final objective from the enemy.

18th July 1916

This order to be read to all troops and then destroyed.

On 21 July General Rawlinson, commanding Fourth Army, sent the following message to 21st Division HQ

Owing to the difficulty of assembling the Division it will not be possible for me to address them personally as I had wished.

I desire, therefore, that my congratulations and thanks may be conveyed to each Officer, N.C.O. and man of the Division for their excellent work and great gallantry during the Battle of the SOMME.

Their two successful assaults against the carefully prepared defences of the enemy's first and second systems is a feat of arms which will rank high in the attainments of the British Army.

No troops could have answered to the call of duty with greater

dash, and the valour of the infantry, coupled with the excellent support afforded by the artillery, is deserving of the highest praise.

Your Corps Commander has repeatedly expressed to me his satisfaction both with the training of the Division before the first assault, and the behaviour of all ranks when in close contact with the enemy.

I regret that the 21st Division is leaving the Fourth Army, but they performed their part in this great battle in a manner that has filled me with admiration, and I trust that at some future time I may again have the honour of finding them under my command.

At 8 am on the 19th 22 Brigade was ordered to extend their front line to include the road from High Wood to Bazentin le Grand, and 1/RWF moved to the new line with 2/Warwicks in support.

The continuing German bombardment of the Caterpillar Valley area with gas and lachrymatory shell, and with increasingly adverse weather conditions interfering with aerial reconnaissance and artillery observation, the preparations for effecting Fourth Army plans, including the early renewal of action against High Wood and the Switch Line, were seriously affected.

Lieutenant Siegfried Sassoon 1/RWF was one of eight officers retained in reserve in the transport lines where he *existed monotonously*, whilst his battalion fought its part in the battle. Being removed from action was not a situation he relished at this time.His account of the battalion returning to bivouac on a hill above Dernancourt when the Division was relieved from the front line, captures perfectly the atmosphere after battle.

An hour before dawn the road was still an empty picture of moonlight. The distant gun-fire had crashed and rumbled all night, muffled and terrific with immense flashes, like waves of some tumult of water rolling along the horizon. Now there came an interval of silence in which I heard a horse neigh, shrill and scared and lonely. Then the procession of returning troops began. The camp fires were burning low when the grinding jolting column lumbered back.. The field guns came first, with nodding men sitting stiffly on weary horses, followed by wagons and limbers and field kitchens. After this rumble of wheels came the infantry, shambling, limping, straggling and out of step. If anyone spoke it was only a muttered word, and the mounted officers rode as if asleep. The men had carried their emergency water in petrol-cans, against which bayonets made a hollow clink; except for the shuffling of feet, this was the only sound.

Reserve officers enjoy scotch and water in the mess. The subaltern on the right wears a Prussian artilleryman's ball topped Pickelhaube.

Then, as if answering our expectancy, a remote skirling of bagpipes began, and the Gordon Highlanders hobbled in. But we had been sitting at the crossroads nearly six hours, and faces were recognisable, when Dottrell hailed our leading Company.

Soon they had dispersed and settled down on the hillside, and were asleep in the daylight which made everything seem ordinary. None the less I had seen something that night which overawed me. It was all in the day's work – an exhausted division returning from the Somme Offensive – but for me it was as though I had watched an army of ghosts. It was as though I had seen the War as it might be envisioned by the mind of some epic poet a hundred years hence.[12]

On 17 July 1916 The Battle of Bazentin Ridge was officially concluded.

The rising ground fronting the newly formed British line between Bazentin le Petit and Longueval reverted to a bloody No Man's Land, and the battles against High Wood and the Switch Line, and for Delville Wood raged on with unabated ferocity.

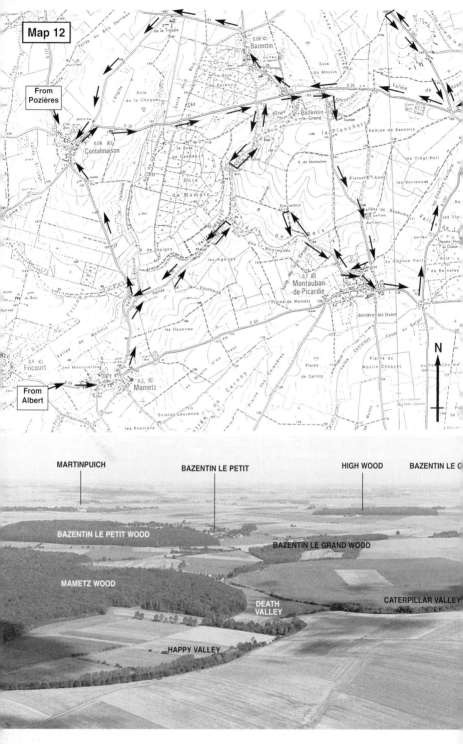

Map 12

From Pozières

Contalmaison

From Albert

Fricourt

Mametz

Montauban-de-Picardie

Bazentin

Bazentin-le-Grand

N

MARTINPUICH　　　BAZENTIN LE PETIT　　　HIGH WOOD　　　BAZENTIN LE G

BAZENTIN LE PETIT WOOD

BAZENTIN LE GRAND WOOD

MAMETZ WOOD

DEATH VALLEY

CATERPILLAR VALLEY

HAPPY VALLEY

Chapter Twelve

A DRIVE AND WALKING TOUR AROUND THE BATTLEFIELD OF BAZENTIN RIDGE

This tour is designed to be a combination of walking and driving; however it can be used as a driving tour alone. The full tour, taking the opportunity to get out and visit memorials and cemeteries, can take as long as a day; but at the least, half a day should be allowed for.

The area in which the Battle of Bazentin Ridge developed and was fought, following the successful breakthrough in the south in the early days of the Somme battle, is easily accessible; and most of the places of action can be viewed conveniently from vantage points surrounding the battlefield. By car it is advisable to stay on the metalled roads which are described on the routes and, as the area is notorious for surface mud, to avoid tracks which are designated for walking only. In case of problems, in my own first-hand experience, M.Chocquet, who runs the garage in Pozières, is a reliable and careful vehicle retriever. On all roads watch closely for the often profuse numbers of farm vehicles, the drivers of which are generally considerate. One should always ensure that a vehicle never blocks the highway, or track; or if it does, that the driver is always within easy reach to move it.

Bear in mind that the woods are private and used for the breeding of game birds, and that rough shooting is a popular sport and eager participants, some of whom are not particularly expert, are frequently encountered. I would especially encourage people to keep out of all woods, regardless of permission being granted, on Sundays from the early autumn until the beginning of spring, ie early March. Even visiting isolated cemeteries can be potentially a little risky, judging from personal experience!

Other books in the Battleground Europe series cover the areas surounding the Bazentins. *Fricourt-Mametz* by Michael Stedman; *High Wood* by Terry Carter; *Mametz Wood* by Michael Renshaw; and *Delville Wood* by Nigel Cave are all excellent complementary guides to action which took place before and after The Battle of Bazentin Ridge, and are recommended to complete the appreciation of the countryside across which this part of the Somme Battle was fought, and to increase the enjoyment of your visit.

To access this route from **Bapaume**, take the **D929** Albert road as far as **Pozières**, and turn left on the **D147** to **Contalmaison**. On entering the village, turn left onto the **D20**. **Contalmaison Chateau cemetery** is signposted to the left, and

Contalmaison Chateau – the ruins in 1917. The graves have been tended and fresh flowers supplied by those French villagers who had returned to the wreckage.

The Red Dragon memorial to the Welsh Division. The Hammerhead to the left, Bazentin le Petit wood in the distance down Death Valley.

a little way beyond, **the route of the tour can be joined in Contalmaison** at the bend where the D147 joins the D20 from the right. The options are either to turn right into the D147 and first left past the pond towards Mametz, and then to continue to the 38th (Welsh) Division memorial which is sign-posted, there to start the tour; or alternatively to continue on the D20 round the bend and pick up the tour route from that point.

To access the route from **Albert**, take the **D938** Peronne road through the village of St. Quentin then turn left onto the **D64** and bear right towards **Mametz**.

A signpost in **Mametz** village will direct you towards the **38th (Welsh) Division Memorial**. At a fork in this road the Memorial is sign posted to the right and runs across the higher ground above **Happy Valley**. On the right was the major trench area of White Trench; on the left was the area known as the **Queen's Nullah**. It was here that Major General EC Ingouville-Williams, commanding the 34th Division, was struck and killed by a shell fragment on 22nd July. The farm track, which runs along the lower level at the base of the escarpment, was the route of **Willow Trench** which was used by troops moving up from Fricourt. A German built narrow gauge railway also ran along the side of the valley to connect at **Bottom Wood** with the line from Martinpuich to Contalmaison. The state of this lower farm track is unreliable and is not suitable for use by cars.

The magnificent modern, **Red Dragon**, sculpture of the memorial commemorates those lost in the well-documented and horrifically bloody struggles of the Welsh New Army brigades which wrested Mametz Wood from the well entrenched defenders during the period 7th to 12th July 1916. The action is fully described in Michael Renshaw's Mametz Wood, in this series.

The road circles around just beyond the memorial for ease of exit, and the welcome addition of steps now allows easy ascent. The memorial is also a fine vantage point from which to view the assembly areas of the battalions moving up for the attacks on Bazentin and High Wood, with Happy Valley stretching out behind and beside Mametz Wood, Death Valley running alongside the Hammerhead towards Flatiron Copse cemetery, and Caterpillar valley starting below the escarpment of Caterpillar Wood just round the corner to the east.

Return to the fork and turn sharp right back onto the **C4** road to **Contalmaison**.

Bottom Wood abuts the road to the left, and the small **Quadrangle Wood** is on the right. **Quadrangle Trench** crossed this road about two hundred yards further on.

172

A fine view of the western side of Mametz Wood and the sweep of the front captured on the 11th /12th July can be seen this point. **Contalmaison (Civilian) Cemetery** is on the right at the top of the rise, where stood the crucifix seen by Lieutenant de Lisle of 9/Leicesters as he peered through the dereliction and carnage, and upon which he commented so eloquently in his diary. At the eastern end of the cemetery, overlooking the site of Acid Drop Copse, stands the memorial to **12/Manchesters**. The Battalion sustained overwhelming losses in an ill-conceived attack in the morning of 7th July against **Quadrangle Support Trench** which ran parallel to, and about one hundred and fifty yards to the right of the road. **Pearl Alley Trench** ran through the cemetery to connect with Quadrangle trench some three hundred yards to the west. On their arrival from the north of the Somme battlefield 7/Leicesters and 9/Leicesters held the front here, occupying these and the trenches over to Mametz Wood, and suffering heavy and sustained bombardments before withdrawing to Fricourt to prepare for the attack on Bazentin.

BELL'S REDOUBT

The memorial to 2/Lt Donald Bell VC.

On the right where the road slopes down, just before Contalmaison, is the recently commissioned and impressive memorial to **Second-Lieutenant DS Bell VC**, 9/Yorks (Green Howards), who was awarded the Victoria Cross on 5th July, and who was killed at this spot on 10th July 1916. The wooden cross replicates that which was erected on his grave at the time, and the position and the poignant impact of this simple memorial is alone worth the visit.

At the T-junction turn right onto the **D147** through **Contalmaison**. A detour a short distance up the road to the left will take you to the site of Contalmaison Chateau and the very attractive military Cemetery. **Private William Short VC**, 8/Yorks, who was awarded the Victoria Cross for action in Munster Trench is buried here.

At the wide T-junction in Contalmaison village continue ahead onto the **D20** and towards Bazentin and Longueval (but note you do not have right of way). After the bend to the right, as you travel down the hill towards the sunken section of the road, stands the dark bulk of **Mametz Wood**. The small woods on the left are on the sites of **Pearl Wood, Lower Wood, Middle Wood**, and **Villa Wood**.

VILLA WOOD   MIDDLE WOOD   PEARL WOOD   BAZENTIN LE PETIT WOOD   LOWER WOOD

Drive along the side of Mametz Wood and stop about a hundred yards before the visible end. The track on the left leading up the west side of Bazentin le Petit Wood was the route of the **narrow gauge railway**, and in 1916 Mametz Wood started to diverge from the road about 200 yards before this point. The German front line trench ran approximately parallel to, and about a hundred yards in front of, Bazentin le Petit Wood. The 110 Brigade troops formed up in attack formation between the two woods, **8/Leicesters** on a one hundred yards front west from the railway, **7/Leicesters** along the front of Mametz Wood, and **6/Leicesters** beyond. On the lift of the ferocious bombardment of the German front lines at 3.25 am on the 14th July 1916 the first wave rose and advanced towards the opposing trenches. In crossing the churned up ground, casualties from machine gun fire were especially concentrated on each flank and midway between here and where the road and Bazentin le Petit Wood now intersect.

The path along the west side of the wood gives a good walking surface to the north of Bazentin village along the flank fought for and held by 8/Leicesters, and tracking the positions of the progressive artillery lifts can be an intriguing aside on a warm and pleasant day.

A hundred yards further on, and a hundred and fifty yards **along the track** into Mametz Wood, lies the grave of **13587 Lance Corporal Harry Fellows** 12/Northumberland Fusiliers, whose ashes are scattered in the wood, and who features in the very moving film 'The Battle of the Somme' at the Museum in Peronne. Although he lived for so many years after the war, he wished to lie with his former comrades. Note that access to visit the headstone does not, so we understand, require permission, but people should stay on the track and not further venture into the wood; and they enter at their own risk.

Continue along the road to the far (south) end of Bazentin le Petit Wood. This point is the right flank of the 110 Brigade front, and from here to the east side of Bazentin le Grand Wood was the 20 and 22 Brigades sector. Turn right down the metalled track signposted to **Flatiron Copse Cemetery**. The **German front line trench**, attacked here by **2/Borders** in the gloom of the morning of 14 July, crossed in front of **Bazentin le Grand Wood** on the left, about seven hundred yards along the track. This wood was not relaid after the cessation of the Great War and still contains traces of trench lines and shelling scars, and although the south edge was extended forwards by about seventy yards the shape is little altered. Difficult now to identify, gaps existed between Bazentin le Grand Wood, **Sabot Copse**, and **Flatiron Copse** on the left of the track, although they are still identifiable from the top of the quite steeply rising ground to the left, the crown of which was wired and fortified and known as **The Snout**.

The attack front of **20 Brigade** started immediately opposite the line of the north-facing wall of **Flatiron Copse Cemetery**. Between here and up the slope to the track north of **Marlborough Wood**, 2/Borders and 8/Devons awaited zero hour in their assault formations, ready to advance on and through Bazentin le Grand Wood.

Flatiron Copse Cemetery started with the burying of the dead from Mametz Wood on 14 July 1916, and rapidly expanded with the additions from the Bazentin battlefield, and subsequently from the surrounding area. There are over 1,500 gravestones, including that of **Sgt Edward Dwyer VC**, 1/East Surrey's, who was

Pioneers beside the shattered Mametz Wood awaiting the order to fall in for the march to Bazentin 17 July, 1916.

awarded the Victoria Cross in the Ypres salient. The identity of many of those buried here is unknown. Of the five hundred Leicesters who perished at Bazentin, less than a hundred were identifiable, the others are remembered by the inscription of their names on the Thiepval Memorial to the Missing.

Flatiron Copse Cemetery. Started in July 1916 many of the dead from the Bazentin Battle are buried here.

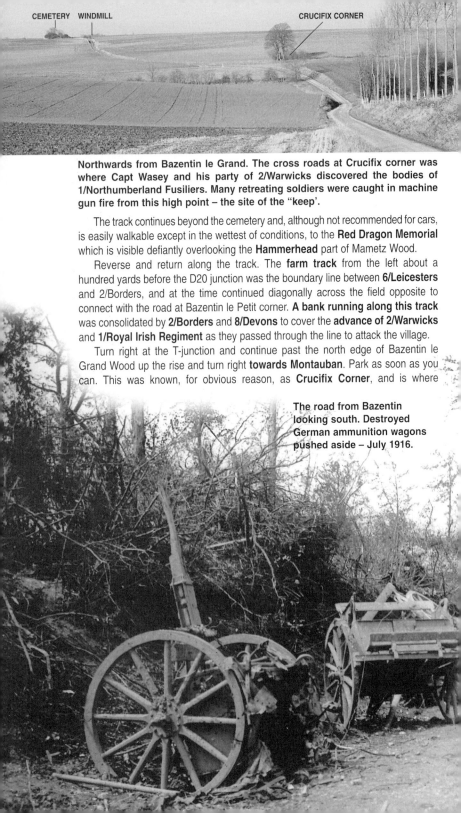

CEMETERY WINDMILL

CRUCIFIX CORNER

Northwards from Bazentin le Grand. The cross roads at Crucifix corner was where Capt Wasey and his party of 2/Warwicks discovered the bodies of 1/Northumberland Fusiliers. Many retreating soldiers were caught in machine gun fire from this high point – the site of the "keep".

The track continues beyond the cemetery and, although not recommended for cars, is easily walkable except in the wettest of conditions, to the **Red Dragon Memorial** which is visible defiantly overlooking the **Hammerhead** part of Mametz Wood.

Reverse and return along the track. The **farm track** from the left about a hundred yards before the D20 junction was the boundary line between **6/Leicesters** and 2/Borders, and at the time continued diagonally across the field opposite to connect with the road at Bazentin le Petit corner. **A bank running along this track** was consolidated by **2/Borders** and **8/Devons** to cover the **advance of 2/Warwicks** and **1/Royal Irish Regiment** as they passed through the line to attack the village.

Turn right at the T-junction and continue past the north edge of Bazentin le Grand Wood up the rise and turn right **towards Montauban**. Park as soon as you can. This was known, for obvious reason, as **Crucifix Corner**, and is where

The road from Bazentin looking south. Destroyed German ammunition wagons pushed aside – July 1916.

Captain Wasey and his patrol discovered the bodies of the **1/Northumberland Fusiliers** and subsequently jointly engaged in action against the German troops entrenched in the ground to the east and along the **fortified gully** now marked by the line of trees where the ground rises towards **Bazentin le Grand village**.

Continue up the hill. The **renovated farm and buildings on the left** are on part of the site of Bazentin le Grand village, which even before the destruction was smaller than le Petit village. At the time of the battle a cluster of houses existed on the right hand side of the road opposite the present farm entrance, and extended forward for about eighty yards. A large farm complex existed where the present buildings now stand, with a number of other houses and buildings behind, the whole being surrounded by orchard and trees extending east from the road by some two hundred and fifty yards, with an important German communications trench running along the eastern boundary.

One hundred yards beyond the farm entrance the **German second line** crossed the road, and the Front line trench was a further hundred yards ahead. On the left a small coppice or orchard ran back as far as where now is the front of the long white barn. Note **from this high ground the view** across the British positions from which the attacks were launched, and the range of fire northwards from the rapidly established British strong points on the ridge once the village and the wood had been secured.

Continue over the crest of the hill to the crossing of the track running east – west. Behind this track crouched the attacking **12/West Yorks** to the right, and **13/King's Liverpools** to the left, the road being the dividing line between the two battalions. 13/King's' front extended eastwards for about a thousand yards to adjoin 7/KSLI (later augmented by 2/Royal Scots) of 8 Brigade.

The cart track to the right, after about eight hundred yards turns left down the hill. At this point the front line German trench, swinging in an arc from in front of Bazentin le Grand with the contour, connected with the track, and then ran in a straight line into the wood. Before the bombardment, the whole of the German front trench was guarded by a double row of barbed wire. This was largely destroyed, but a stretch remained undamaged in 8 Brigade sector adjoining 13/King's, which

Quarry Cemetery beside the Bazentin le Grand - Montauban road started in 1916 at the site of an advance dressing station. Bernafay wood in the background.

CATERPILLAR WOOD   MARLBOROUGH WOOD   BAZENTIN LE PETIT WOOD   BAZENTIN LE GRAND WOOD

The panoramic view of the battlefield from Montauban.

seriously impeded progress and caused problems to the assault against the eastern flank of Bazentin le Grand.

The track, at a point about four hundred yards up from Marlborough Wood, visible south-west across the slope towards Caterpillar Wood, **was the boundary** between the **7th and 3rd Divisions** and where lines of **8/Devons** and **12/West Yorks** met.

Continue down the slope. The **bottom of the valley** was where the troops of the 3rd and 7th Divisions assembled and support battalions awaited their moves forward, and the area became extensively filled with stores and dumps, and wheel to wheel artillery batteries after the first day's advances.

To the left of the road in the valley **Quarry Cemetery** is clearly visible. A pause here is well worthwhile. At the time of the battle this was the site of an Advanced Dressing Station, and the burials here started at that time and continued until February 1917, after which bodies were brought in for burial from other parts of the battlefield.

Proceed up the hill to **Montauban**, take the first right, then right again. The elevated ground here gives a **fine panoramic view** of the rear areas from the British perspective. To the west, on the high ground above **Caterpillar valley**, were the sites of the **British machine gun emplacements** which raked fire across the German positions on the other side of the valley. Between Mametz Wood to the left, and Bazentin le Grand Wood, the ground over which 110 (Leicestershire) Brigade advanced is clearly visible in the distance, the up-slopes west of Marlborough Wood was where the 2/Borders and the 8/Devons attacked, and to the right of Marlborough Wood the front of 12/West Yorks and 13/King's (Liverpool), and

CATERPILLAR WOOD   MAMETZ WOOD

CATERPILLAR VALLEY

continuing east, up towards where **Caterpillar Valley Cemetery** now stands on the horizon, the Scottish battalions of the **9th Division** advanced. Continuing down this road will take you across Caterpillar Valley, with Caterpillar Wood on the escarpment to your left, and **up the sunken road to Marlborough Wood**. The metalled track is unsuitable for cars beyond this point, and you will need to reverse and return along this road to Montauban.

On reaching the T-junction opposite the white capped gateposts, turn right, then left at the next, by the church, onto the **D64**. The recently erected memorial to the **Manchester and Liverpool Pals**, who fought through to the village on 1 July, stands on the right of the road.

Continue along the D64 to the cross roads and turn left on the **D197** snaking down the hill towards **Longueval**. On the right stands **Bernafay Wood** with its **cemetery** opposite on the site of an Advanced Dressing Station established on 4 July after capture by the 9th (Scottish) Division. The long wood to the east is the much disputed Trones Wood, eventually secured by the British on the morning of 14 July, and where **Sgt. William Boulter**, 6/Northamptons, earned his Victoria Cross.

Just before Longueval on the right is the small triangular **Longueval Road Cemetery**, which was from where 8/Black Watch attacked Longueval on 14 July. From this point the whole sweep of the eastern end of the battlefront is visible, from Delville Wood to Trones Wood, then Bernafay Wood, Montauban church, and Caterpillar Valley running away to the treetops at Caterpillar Wood with Mametz Wood behind, and the white barn at Bazentin le Grand standing on the crest of the ridge silhouetted against the backdrop of the Bazentin Woods.

Should **a refreshment break be required**, there is a Bar and the Café Calypso both under the able and personal direction of M.Blondel either side of the cross roads in Longueval or, after a right turn at the cross roads and a left after five hundred yards you will arrive at the **Visitor Centre at Delville Wood, with the South African National Memorial and Museum** a short distance beyond.

Memorial cairn to the men of the Highland Light infantry killed 15 July, 1916. Built from stones from Scotland, one for each man.

To continue the tour, turn left at the crossroads in Longueval onto the **D20** to Contalmaison.

For an optional and interesting **diversion to High Wood**, turn first right on the **D107** to Martinpuich. Continue along this road to High Wood. The track on the right before the wood leads, after a walk (or drive – the track quality is good and there is ample turning space) of some four hundred yards, to the 1/Cameron Highlanders and Black Watch memorial.

The Memorials on the right of the road fronting the wood are to: the 47th London Division; then a small plaque identifies the oak tree planted in memory of 20/Royal Fusiliers (Public Schools Battalion); and then the Memorial Cairn to the men of **9/Highland Light Infantry** who died in the attack on the 15th July.

The **London Cemetery and Extension** stands to the left of the

Panoramic view from Marlborough Wood.

BAZENTIN LE PETIT WOOD   BAZENTIN LE GRAND WOOD

road, and is a good place to park. This cemetery contains over 3300 graves, mostly of unknown soldiers, whose remains were buried here from the surrounding battlefields. The burial ground was first used by the 47th Division in September 1916 when forty seven bodies were interred here in a large shell hole. A walk through the cemetery is recommended, to the **south edge** which commands **a fine view of the battle field from the German perspective**. On the left is the village of Longueval, then on the ridge to the right Caterpillar Valley cemetery. Slightly to the right again, on the line of Montauban church which is clearly identifiable on the horizon, was where the **cavalry** charged up the slope to attack High Wood on the evening of 14 July. Bazentin le Grand Wood is directly ahead, with the site of the **windmill** on top of the rise in front of it, and Bazentin le Petit village and wood is to the right across the front of the aborted attack by the 100 Brigade, westward against the Switch Line, of 15 July. On the horizon to the right is the red and white radio mast at Poziéres which serves as a focal point all around the Somme battlefields.

Return towards Longueval to continue the tour and **turn right at the D20**. After a short distance, on the left, is the very large **Caterpillar Valley Cemetery** containing about 5200 graves, and many special memorials, including one of the New Zealand Memorials to the Missing. The ridge here was captured by the 9th Division on 14 July. A little further along the road on the opposite side is the signpost to **Thistle Dump Cemetery**. The farm track indicated, which is only for walking, continues on past the grass path leading to the small **attractive** cemetery and, parallel to, and immediate left of the track, is the front over which the **cavalry charged**, pennants flying and lances glinting, up the slope to High Wood on the evening of 14 July.

On approaching **Crucifix Corner** again note on the **right a farm track**. This was also the **start of the trench used by Lt Beadle** to access the **forward observation position in front of the Windmill**, but in which he, after about a hundred yards, became disorientated in the network of wrecked trenchwork and entered in error the German communication trench leading up the slope towards High Wood. There he met and shot the German soldier, and stayed to inadvertently witness the cavalry charge at close quarters.

Continue on to the bottom of the hill and bear right at what was known as **Six Ways Corner** on the D73 into Bazentin le Petit. Park somewhere beside the church which is directly ahead. The church entrance before 1916 faced the Lamarck House – the present church rebuilt in a much improved style is reversed – the entrance faces the village. On the left, the modern sculpture representing the Giraffe is a tribute to **Jean Baptiste Lamarck**, the celebrated and revolutionary naturalist, botanist, scientist, zoologist and philosopher who was born in Bazentin le Petit in 1744, and an acknowledged inspiration to the later Charles Darwin. The **Lamarck house** stood on the site of where now stands the memorial bust behind the church,

Lamarck House – the birthplace of Jean-Baptiste Lamarck. The ruined back view before final destruction.

in grounds which became known as the **Clearing**, and ironically the very epicentre of the battles of 1916 in, and revolving around, Bazentin le Petit. The **large house**, bounded now by the low wall surrounding the monument, was used as **a German field hospital** before the battlefront encroached and the building was wrecked.

Beside the church stands the memorial to the villagers who died in the Great War. The tranquil grassed area at the corner opposite, where now grows chestnut trees, was the site of a **German field battery**.

Bazentin le Petit was completely destroyed during the attacks and counterattacks and the attendant bombardments. The northern segment of the clearing, viewed easily from the Lamarck monument, is where the **Leicestershire Brigade** was severely mauled, and where **2/RIR** met the counter-attacking German force from the north east of the wood. The number of British soldiers killed and wounded in the village and wood on 14 July 1916 alone is estimated at two thousand four hundred, with an additional thousand at Bazentin le Grand. The German losses can be assumed to be at least similar.

Opposite the church, **Rue Neuve** gives road access to the civil and **Military Cemetery**, which was started in July 1916 and contains the graves of many of the 1/Northamptonshire Regiment who died in August 1916. Next to this cemetery is the **Quarry** which became the HQ of various Brigades and was where the injured **Captain Robert Graves** was brought and lay whilst being pronounced as 'Died of Wounds'. From the back of the small coppice behind the cemetery the site of the **windmill** is clearly indicated by the crowns of a small stand of trees on the crest of the rise.

Just four hundred yards to the north-west of the cemetery was where, as result of conspicuous bravery during an assault on the Intermediate Trench on the 30 July by 5/SWB and 81 Field Company RE, **Private James Miller 7/King's Own Royal Lancaster** was posthumously awarded the Victoria Cross. His citation tells that he 'was ordered to take an important message under heavy shell fire and rifle fire and to bring back a reply at all costs. He was compelled to cross the open, and on leaving the trench was shot almost immediately in the back, the bullet coming out through his abdomen. In spite of this, with heroic courage and self sacrifice, he compressed with his hand the gaping wound in his abdomen, delivered his message, staggered back with the answer, and fell at the feet of the officer to whom he delivered it. He gave his life with a supreme devotion to duty'. Born at Hoghton, near Preston, in 1890, his body is buried in **Dartmoor Cemetery**, **Becordel**.

Return to the Church and proceed northwards along the main road. On the left

Bazentin le Petit communal and military cemetery with the quarry behind. The quarry served as brigade HQ and later an advanced dressing centre and was where the seriously wounded Robert Graves was pronounced dead.

is sign posted **Bazentin le Petit Military Cemetery**. The approach footpath stands on the **line of the shallow trench to which the 6/Leicesters fell back** when the **2/RIR** were driven from the north of the village on the morning of 14th, and from where they were subsequently driven by intense shelling and counter-attack to regroup across the clearing. The **area of the wood behind the cemetery** was the scene of fierce fighting throughout the 14th as the Leicestershire Brigade struggled to wrest the north west corner from the German occupants, and were assailed by counter-attacks from the north. The bloodshed continued here unabated on the 15th as machine guns wreaked their havoc from **the strong point north west of the wood**, and a heavily fortified trench just outside the wood.

To investigate the north end, park where convenient near the road intersection at the top of the village. A short way along the minor road to Martinpuich directly ahead, is where **Robert Graves** collected his memento for **Dr JC Dunn** from a shattered gun carriage. The **road to the right**, leads to the (often muddied) sunken road up to the corner of High Wood. From the line of this track the **unsuccessful assault** was launched against the **Switch Line Trench** on the 15th July 1916, by the 1/Queen's, 9/HLI, 1/Middlesex and 16/KRRC, and is where **Robert Graves** saw the corpses of the **Glasgow Highlanders** huddled against the left bank. After about two hundred yards, on the top of the bank stands, a calvary, the memorial to Capt. HSH Wallace, 10/Worcesters, who died here on the morning

The church at Bazentin le Petit (left) in 1916, (bottom) the temporary church after the war and (right) the rebuilt church today.

Before the battle. A ration wagon for the Germans billetted in Bazentin, 1915. The church can be seen in the background.

of 22 July 1916. This was recently restored in a cooperative effort by the village and the Western Front Association.

Just beyond the memorial on the right are two farm tracks, the first leading directly to the **Quarry and cemetery**, the second to Bazentin le Grand passing the site of the **windmill**, which stood where the isolated group of trees now stands. Both paths are walkable but stout footware is recommended especially when underfoot conditions are not absolutely dry. From this corner the upward sweep of country across which the senior officers walked in the mid-morning of the 14 July to reconnoitre High Wood can be appreciated. At the centre front of High Wood the London Cemetery and Extension is clearly visible.

On returning to the road intersection at the top of the village, you will see the memorial to sappers killed in Bazentin le Petit between the 29th to 31st January 1916 **and dedicated 'To Nine Brave Men'**. Constructed using bricks reclaimed from the ruins of the village, this memorial was built, by **Major R.F. Butterworth**, the Commanding Officer of 82/Field Engineer Company RE. on his return to the site later in the war. During the

The Lamarck memorial stands behind the church on the site of Lamark House, used as a German field hospital before the battle. Destroyed during the action, the house was never rebuilt.

Calvary to the memory of Captain HSH Wallace 10/Worcester who was killed 22 July, 1916 at Bazentin le Petit and whose name is inscribed on the memorial to the missing at Thiepval. The calvary was first erected in 1923 and was most recently restored in 1994.

time when his companies, working under orders from 57 Brigade (19 Division), were engaged in vital work around Bazentin le Petit they volunteered to continue under extremely dangerous conditions until the nine men commemorated had been killed and nearly all others wounded.

The track to the left of the memorial towards the **north-east corner** of Bazentin le Petit Wood, which in 1916 continued on to **Contalmaison Villa**, was a final objective of the **110 Brigade**. Numerous attempts to capture and consolidate this road cost many lives.

Walk down this track as far as the corner of the wood. Across the small field to the left, the line of the fence across to the north east corner of the wood was that held by **6/Leicesters** on the evening of 14 July. Thirty yards to the right of the track and swinging round in an arc some forty or fifty yards in front of the north edge of the wood, was the **resolutely defended German trench** from which so much damage was caused to the attacking British. Some twenty yards in front of the track running along the north edge of the wood is where **Captain Emmett and his thirty-six men**, attempting to storm the trench, were killed and their bodies never found. The point where the track meets the wood is where the **tramway** entered and which, into the wood for about one hundred yards, was the boundary of the north west portion of the wood, strongly attacked and desperately defended at great cost to both sides throughout the 14th. From the evening of the 14th the north edge of the wood was held by **7/Leicesters, 9/Leicesters, and 1/East Yorks, 8/Leicesters** held the western edge, and **6/Leicesters** the line from the wood to the village.

The final loop of the tour will take us back to Contalmaison. Continue along the D20 in the direction of Poziéres. After about four hundred yards the **narrow gauge railway** crossed this road on its way from Martinpuich through Bazentin le Petit Wood and Mametz Wood to Bottom Wood, and a hundred yards further on, where the farm track crosses the road (although this is sometimes under plough and difficult to locate) and about 200 yards to the left, is **the site of the large fortified strong point** which posed such great problems to the commanders of the attacking British, held them at bay, and from where so many were killed.

Continue for another five hundred yards and turn down the track to the left immediately after the **Ferme de la Trouee**. The German front line trench (**Villa Trench**) crossed this track about five hundred yards along, running eastwards to continue into what was known as **Flatiron Trench** on the south side of Bazentin le Petit Wood, and continuing on the right to the north of Poziéres. After another five hundred yards on the left is the site of the **German strong point at Contalmaison Villa**. A brief stop here will illustrate the vulnerability to machine gun fire from the villa of **8/Leicesters' advance** on the left flank of the British attack at 3.25 am on 14 July.

A right turn at the next T-junction will take you back on to the D20 and into Contalmaison, thence to La Boisselle and onto the D929 Albert – Bapaume road.

Alternatively continue straight on at the junction in Contalmaison (priority from your right) onto the D147 to Fricourt passing Peake Wood Cemetery on the right, then the German Cemetery and Fricourt Wood on the left, through Fricourt and right on to the D938 to Albert.

Chapter Thirteen

WALKS AROUND THE BAZENTINS AND THE BATTLEFIELD AREA

The walks could be combined as a whole or in part with the route of the drive around the battlefield. A study of the maps will enable suitable parking places to be identified, and the walk selected according to plans and time available.

The area can be covered by walking in a rough figure of eight, parking for which can be at a number of places depending upon the duration and type of walk required. On only a short stretch, between Marlborough Wood and Mametz Wood, are difficult underfoot conditions likely to be encountered except in very extreme conditions, although the track between the 38th (Welsh) Division Dragon Memorial and Flatiron Copse cemetery is very uneven. Please remember that the woods are private property and unauthorised access is not allowed. The main points of interest have already been described in detail in the previous chapters or in the drive around the area, and the comments are generally directed at those parts for walkers only. Allow

Map 13: The walking tours around the Bazentin battlefield.

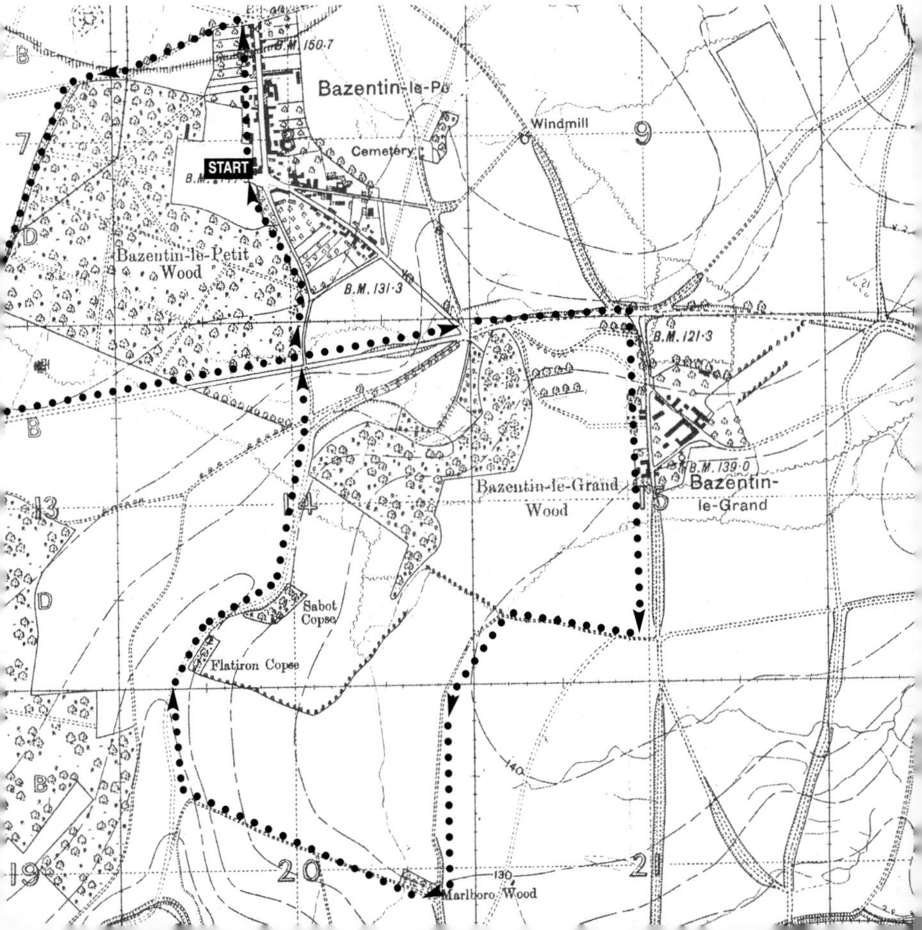

Signs of the conflict. A barbed wire picket enveloped by the trunk of a chestnut tree on the site of the artillery battery opposite the church.

a full half-day for each of the circuits, and be reminded that distance on foot is often far greater than that viewed on map or from car. Refreshment stops are non-existent, a flask and baguette could fill a welcome break.

For the sake of convenience start the route of the walk at Bazentin le Petit church. From the church take the road to the north of the village passing the Mairie on the right. The Military Cemetery, which is sign posted, is to the left some fifty yards along a grass path. Gaps between headstones occur where the bodies of German soldiers were exhumed to be reburied at Fricourt. At the junction of roads, the route is the left fork at the RE Memorial, details of which are recorded in the drive section. This is the track which runs along the north and then the west side of the wood.

A small detour of about six hundred yards along the metalled track opposite, is well worth the effort. This indicates the north boundary of the village and continues up to High Wood. The memorial to Capt Wallace dates from 1923, and the view across the escarpment from the north east corner gives a very good perspective of the distances which needed to be covered, mostly on foot, to launch the attacks on High Wood and the Switch line trenches.

The memorial to the village war dead. Beside the church in Bazentin village.

Continuing along the track to and alongside the wood. The positions of the German strong point and trenches covering the north of the wood have already been identified, but a quick look at the car route will refresh the details. Continue along the west side of the wood. About two hundred yards before the south west corner of the wood, the railway exited and continued along this pathway to enter Mametz Wood directly ahead. A hundred yards beyond the railway exit, Forest Trench emerged to become Aston Trench, and the German front line trench (Flatiron) crossed some fifty yards in front of the wood to continue westwards as Villa Trench. The bombers of the 1/Loyal North Lancs fought along

Bazentin le Petit Military Cemetery. The north east segment was the scene of some of the bloodiest struggles of 14 July. The sole burial here from the battle was Private Hockley who died 17 July, 1916.

these trenches westwards from the 15 July. German troops escaping towards Martinpuich had great difficulty in avoiding the machine gun fire from strong posts sited alongside the wood.

This side of the wood, which was the left flank of the attack, was the responsibility of 8/Leicesters, whose commanding officer, Lieutenant Colonel Mignon, was killed in action just outside the south-west corner early on the morning of 14 July. From this corner one can appreciate the vulnerability of the assault platoons, which were exposed to machine gun fire from Contalmaison Villa (in the direction of the red and white Poziéres tower clearly visible to the west).

On reaching the road turn left, not forgetting that traffic approaches from the opposite direction to that we might normally expect. After a short distance, on the right side of the road, a track enters Mametz Wood and a little way inside on the right stands the memorial headstone to Lance Corporal Harry Fellows. He served with 12/Northumberland Fusiliers, survived and died in 1987 aged 91 years, and his ashes are scattered in this wood in which he fought. He features in an evocative film regularly shown in the *Historial* in Peronne.

Back on the road we are walking across where 110 (Leicestershire) Brigade stormed the German front trench which ran along the length, and about one hundred yards in front, of Bazentin le Petit Wood. 7/Leicesters covered the first six hundred yards of the front, the rest by 6/Leicesters, many of whom were cut down by flank machine gun fire from the north of Bazentin le Grand Wood which can be seen directly ahead. At the end of the wood a left turn will return you to the church along the lane which served as the dividing line between the 21st Division (6/Leicesters) and the 7th Division (2/Warwicks and 2/RIR).

To continue on the **second circuit** of the walk proceed directly along the road. Forest trench (the German second line) emerged from the wood some thirty yards up the lane to the left, became known as Circus trench and curled round in an arc across the road and into Bazentin le Grand Wood some three hundred yards ahead. Here this trench became the 'one hour line' for the artillery lift, which then continued in a straight line from the point of entry of the trench into the wood, to, and through, the village of Bazentin le Grand.

Continue past the road junction, then known as Six Ways Corner, and up the slope. The ditch on the right of the road was the route of Capt Wasey's patrol to Crucifix corner, from where Bazentin le Grand is clearly visible, and where we shall turn right down the road towards Montauban.

Note on the left the gully, now tree-lined, which in July 1916 was fortified with dugouts. This area was the scene of the joint attack, by 2/Warwicks and 1/Northumberlands with Stokes mortars and bombers, against the last defenders of Bazentin le Grand on the morning of the 14th. The buildings of the village were more extensive than now, the houses not being rebuilt following the destruction, and only the (now renovated) farm stands on its original site. In the house to house battle this was doggedly defended, until Lieutenant Lynch and his bombers of 1/Northumberland Fusiliers stormed and eventually captured the surviving occupants in the cellars.

The crucifix at Crucifix Corner.

The German second line trench crossed the road at right angles at the crest of the hill, and the front line was about a hundred yards further on. From their elevated positions in the buildings which stood forward of the present farm entrance and on both sides of the road, the German gunners, although under bombardment, inflicted severe losses on the assaulting battalions of 9 Brigade.

Continue on over the brow of the hill and turn right at the farm track four hundred yards ahead. The forward platoons of 12/West Yorks assembled in their attack positions against the track on this side of the road, 13/King's Liverpools on the other side, and crept forward closer to the German line under the barrage. Upon rising and advancing up the slope many perished in a torrent of machine gun and rifle fire, and many more in over-running the German line and into the curtain of shell fire.

This part of the walk commands a good view across the rear areas of the battlefield. Longueval in the east, across the east of Caterpillar valley to Bernafay Wood, Montauban and the distinctive bulk of its church, the start of Caterpillar Wood as it snakes its way down the valley with Marlborough Wood in the foreground, and on over the rise to Happy Valley and Mametz Wood.

At the bend in the track the German front line trench continued straight on into the wood. Carry on down the track as far as Marlborough Wood on the right and take the farm track immediately behind and to the right. 8/Devons and 2/Borders attacked from positions some five hundred yards up the slope to the right of this track. The valley here to the left was particularly heavily shelled during the period before the battle, although not during the assembly on the night of the 13/14 July, and afterwards the artillery batteries which filled the valley became targets.

The track from here towards the Hammerhead has been known to disappear under the plough, but keep on straight ahead and at a point about eight or nine hundred yards from Marlborough Wood you will meet the track which runs down Death Valley to Bazentin le Petit. On meeting this track, to the left the Red Dragon of the 38th (Welsh) Division stands overlooking the wood and is well worth a visit. The ground between here and the Hammerhead directly ahead is the scene of the terrible slaughter of the first unsuccessful attack by 115 Brigade on the 7th July 1916, which heralded the carnage in which the Welsh battalions became embroiled in their efforts to capture and consolidate Mametz Wood. (See Michael Renshaw's *Mametz Wood* in this series for full details.)

To the right, along our route, stands Flatiron Copse Cemetery, which was started in July 1916 and contains many of the dead of Mametz Wood and of the Battle of Bazentin Ridge. Along this route passed many of the battalions moving forward to fight towards High Wood. The peace of today contrasts starkly with accounts in 1916 of the roadsides being stacked high with debris and dead, the frantic haste and noise of artillery, and the endless tramp and shouts of the troops.

A walk back to Bazentin le Petit along this track will take you past Flatiron Copse, Sabot Copse, and Bazentin le Grand Wood, although the breaks between them are now difficult to see.

To the left, fronting Mametz Wood, is where the 110 (Leicestershire) Brigade assembled to attack, at 3.25 am on 14 July 1916, the wood of Bazentin le Petit which is ahead and to the left. On crossing the main road at the end of the track, the lane alongside Bazentin le Petit Wood will deliver you back to the church.

BIBLIOGRAPHY

Public Records Office Kew.Official Papers.
WO 153 to 183 Battle of Bazentin Ridge.

WO 95	921	XV Army Corps Diaries	General Staff
	923		Adjutant and QMS
	925		Command RA
	925		Command Heavy Artillery
	928		Medical Services
	929 to 933		CRE and Ordnance
	1231	1st Division Diary General Staff	
	1377	3rd Division Diary General Staff	
	1392	3rd Division Diary C.R.A.	
	1416	Brigade Diary	8 Brigade
	1426	Brigade Diary	9 Brigade
	1631	7th Division Diary	
	1645	War Diary	95/Field Company RE
	1646	War Diary	24/Manchesters (Pioneers)
	1653	Brigade Diary	20 Brigade
	1655	War Diary	8/Devons
	1655	War Diary	2/Borders
	1656	War Diary	9/Devons
	1656	War Diary	2/Gordon Highlanders
	1660	Brigade Diary	22 Brigade
	1662	War Diary	2/RIR
	1663	War Diary	20/Manchesters
	1664	War Diary	2/Royal Warwicks
	1665	War Diary	1/RWF -7/MGC -22MGC.
	2069	War Diary	82 Field Company RE
	2130	21st Division Diary	
	2144	War Diary	97/Field Company RE
	2144		98/Field Company RE
	2144		126/Field Company RE
	2146		14/Nthumberland Fusiliers
	2151	Brigade Diary	62 Brigade
	2152	21st Division Diary Addendum	
	2155	War Diary	12/Northumberland Fusiliers
	2156	War Diary	10/Yorks
	2159	Brigade Diary	64 Brigade
	2161	War Diary	1/East Yorks
	2163	Brigade Diary	110 Brigade
	2164	War Diary	6/Leicesters
	2165	War Diary	110 MGC.
	2405	33rd Division Diary	
Map Room		German dispositions 1 – 14 July 1916.	
		German Army Orders 12 – 21 July 1916.	

Diary of RQMS Cave. 7th Battalion Leicestershire Regiment. Private Papers [1]
Memoirs of 17411 Pte J W Horner 6/Leicesters Private papers. [2]
Extracts from Chapter 3, Kitcheners Army D.A.Bacon, late B.Q.M.S. 110 Brigade.
Dedicated to Fallen Comrades. Private Papers [3]
Letter from CSM Ben Stafford 8/Leics to Captain F. Ward 8/Leics. Private Papers. [4]
Old Soldiers Never Die. Frank Richards DCM MM. Faber and Faber 1933. [5]
39 months with the Tigers. D.V.Kelly M.C. Ernest Benn Ltd., London.[6]
Of Those We Loved. I.L.Read The Pentland Press 1994.[7]
Diary of Lieutenant ACN DeLisle. Squire de Lisle, Quenby Hall. Private Papers.[8]
SOMME. Lyn Macdonald Penguin Books Ltd., 1993.[9]
Somme Harvest. Giles E.M.Eyre The London Stamp Exchange Ltd.,1991.[10]
Goodbye to all That. Robert Graves Cassell & Co Ltd 1929.[11]
Memoirs of an Infantry Officer. Siegfried Sassoon. Faber & Faber Ltd., 1930.[12]
The War the Infantry Knew. Captain J.C.Dunn. P.S.King Ltd. 1938. Abacus 1994.[13]

INDEX